Arts: A second-level course
Understanding Music: Elements, Techniques a[nd...]

UNIT 9
FOLLOWING A SCORE I

UNIT 10
FORMAL PRINCIPLES I

The Open University

UNIT 9 FOLLOWING A SCORE I	**1**
UNIT 10 FORMAL PRINCIPLES I	**29**
REFERENCE MATERIAL	**49**

The Open University, Walton Hall, Milton Keynes MK7 6AA

First published 1994. Reprinted 1998, 1999

Copyright © 1994 The Open University

All rights reserved. No part of this publication may be reproduced, stored in a retrieval system or transmitted in any form or by any means without written permission from the publisher or without a licence from the Copyright Licensing Agency Ltd. Details of such licences (for photographic reproduction) may be obtained from the Copyright Licensing Agency Ltd of 90 Tottenham Court Road, London W1P 9HE.

Edited, designed and typeset by the Open University.

Printed in the United Kingdom by Selwood Printing Ltd., Burgess Hill, West Sussex.

This text forms part of an Open University second-level course. If you would like a copy of *Studying with the Open University*, please write to the Central Enquiry Service, PO Box 200, The Open University, Walton Hall, Milton Keynes, MK7 6YZ. If you have not already enrolled on the course and would like to buy this or other Open University material, please write to Open University Educational Enterprises Ltd, 12 Cofferidge Close, Stony Stratford, Milton Keynes MK11 1BY, United Kingdom.

ISBN 0 7492 1119 9

1.3

UNIT 9

FOLLOWING A SCORE I

Prepared for the Course Team by David Rowland

CONTENTS

1	**CONTENTS AND AIMS**	4
2	**KEYBOARD SCORES I: FINDING 'LANDMARKS'**	5
2.1	BEETHOVEN'S FIFTH SYMPHONY	5
2.2	BACH'S POLONAISE	6
2.3	ARPEGGIOS AND BROKEN CHORDS	9
2.4	OPTIONAL EXERCISE	9
3	**KEYBOARD SCORES II: TEXTURE AND DYNAMICS**	10
4	**LARGER SCORES**	13
4.1	THE ORCHESTRA	13
4.2	INTRODUCING FIGURED BASS AND THE CONTINUO	18
4.3	THE CONTINUO	19
5	**SOLO SONATAS WITH CONTINUO**	21
6	**TRIO SONATAS**	24
7	**SUMMARY**	27

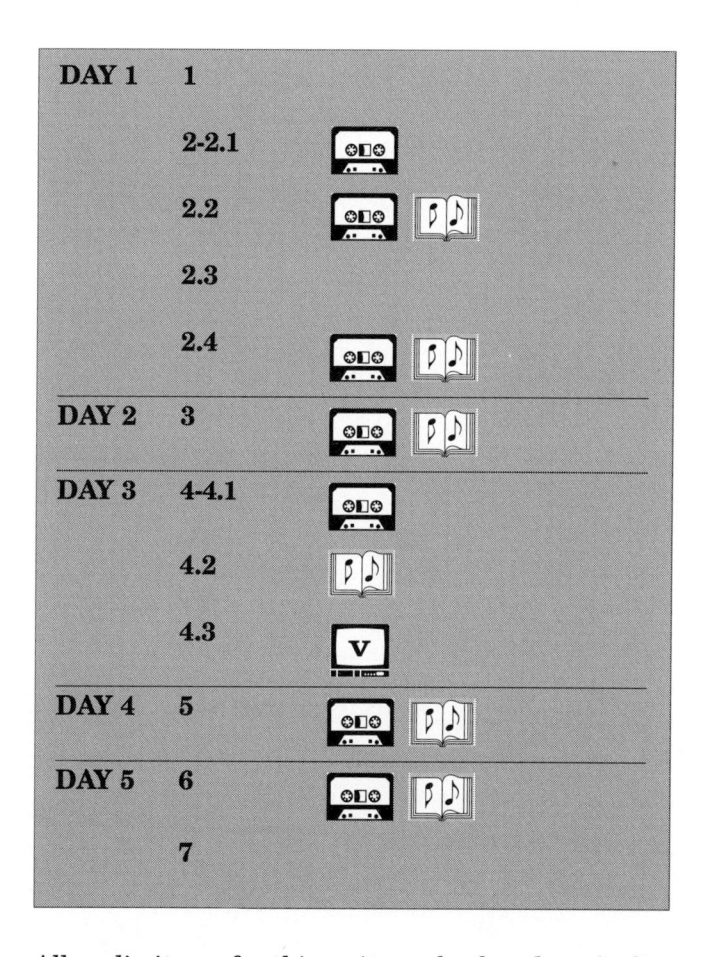

DAY 1	1	
	2–2.1	🎧
	2.2	🎧 📖
	2.3	
	2.4	🎧 📖
DAY 2	3	🎧 📖
DAY 3	4–4.1	🎧
	4.2	📖
	4.3	📺
DAY 4	5	🎧 📖
DAY 5	6	🎧 📖
	7	

All audio items for this unit can be found on Audio-cassette 4.

The video item is on Video-cassette 2.

Score items are in Scores 1 and Scores 2.

1 CONTENT AND AIMS

So far in this course you have concentrated on different aspects of music in turn and you should now be familiar with its important elements. Many of the skills you have learned already will need to be practised and extended, and when you look ahead to the titles of later units you will see how they return to subjects such as 'harmony' and 'melody'. The titles of other units which you will be studying in the next few weeks, however, will be less familiar, though in fact the seeds of most of these topics have been sown in the first part of the course. Score reading is one of these. Apart from a few exercises of a very preliminary nature, you have not so far considered the subject; yet it is, in fact, a skill that you have been learning from week 1 of the course.

Score reading is simply what the term suggests – reading from a musical score – and you can go about it in several ways, just as you can read the written word in several ways. For example, you can read a musical score or the written word silently to yourself, or you can perform it out loud. You might also follow the text while someone else performs it or you might look ahead to anticipate what is about to happen. Whichever method you choose will depend on your reason for doing so. You might wish to scan through the text quickly in silence to get an overall impression of the piece, or you may wish to listen to it and follow the text at the same time so as to get to grips with detail that you might otherwise miss. There are many other possibilities, but whichever way you choose to read a text, practice and experience in one method of reading will invariably improve your technique in another.

So far almost all of your score reading has been with a view to playing short examples on your keyboard – one of the approaches that I have just described. This unit, however, concentrates on a different technique; other people will be performing, while you follow the music in a score. At the end of it you will not necessarily be able to follow every single note in a score as it is played, but you should be able to follow the main 'events' in the music, and quite a lot of the details too. The more you practise, the more detail you will be able to take in. For most of the time you will need your cassette player, the unit texts and the Scores 2 booklet. Your keyboard will be needed only to accompany a short section of video at the end of Section 4 (which you could do earlier in the week if necessary).

The aim of this unit is to help you to read scores of short movements with up to three staves using the treble and bass clefs (although some exercises go a little beyond that for reasons which will become clear). This will enable you to begin to discover some aspects of music that would be difficult to appreciate just by listening. This doesn't mean that listening to music is about to become unimportant in the course; rather, it means that by listening *and* following the music in a score at the same time, you will be able to build up a more complete picture of how music works. Since this is the aim of the course as a whole, it follows that later units will depend on your ability to follow a score. It is therefore important that you *allow plenty of time to practise the exercises in this unit*. The written text is deliberately more brief than in some earlier units to allow you to do so.

2 KEYBOARD SCORES I: FINDING 'LANDMARKS'

2.1 BEETHOVEN'S FIFTH SYMPHONY

Before you look at Example 1, play audio-cassette Item 1. It is the theme from the last movement of Beethoven's Fifth Symphony with the fundamental bass, given in Unit 7, played on the piano.

LISTEN NOW TO ITEM 1.

Now that you have reminded yourself of the theme, we are going to look at Example 1 – the written form of what you have just heard.

Example 1

The extract can be divided into short sections, defined by changes in rhythmic and pitch patterns. Certain individual notes are also important for various reasons. These features can be identified by a brief symbol (for example, 'r' for a change in rhythm, a circle around an important note or rhythm, etc.). By including 'signposts' such as these you will make it easier for yourself to follow the score next time the piece is played. Mark in the following, using symbols that you have chosen for yourself:

- Bar 4 (the end of the first phrase). Both bass and treble parts adopt new rhythmic patterns – the bass part begins a series of semibreves lasting several bars, while the top part has dotted rhythms before rising to the high C in bar 8.

- Bar 8. The treble part reaches a high C for the first time and stays on it for two and a half beats before jumping back down an octave.
- Bar 10. Another top C.
- Bar 12 (last beat). The rhythm of the treble part changes from fairly regular quavers to a more complex rhythm. At the same time, the melody line becomes less smooth.
- Bar 18. Fourth beat: the first time we have heard a group of semiquavers in this extract.
- Bar 22. The semiquavers disappear and a generally downward-moving pattern of quavers begins (which you could indicate with arrows).

On audio-cassette Item 2 you will hear this extract played again, but this time I have identified the beginning of each bar by speaking its number over the sound of the music. This will help you in the initial stages to be sure that you are following the music in the right place. But as you listen to Item 2 again, try to rely less on the bar numbers and concentrate on identifying the 'signposts' that you have marked in your score.

Set your cassette counter to zero so that you can easily return to the beginning of the example and then listen to Item 2 several times, following the music in Example 1.

LISTEN TO ITEM 2 WHILE FOLLOWING EXAMPLE 1.

Now go on to Item 3, which is the same extract without bar numbers (that is, it is a repeat of Item 1). This time you will have to rely entirely on the 'signposts' in Example 1.

LISTEN TO ITEM 3 WHILE FOLLOWING EXAMPLE 1 AND REPEAT IF NECESSARY.

2.2 BACH'S POLONAISE

Example 1 was a transcription of an orchestral work for keyboard. It was played on a piano simply for the sake of convenience. The next piece of music is different. It is the Polonaise in G major, printed in the Scores 2 booklet (p.8), and was originally written for the keyboard by Johann Sebastian Bach (1685–1750). It appears in a collection of instruction pieces compiled for his wife, Anna Magdalena, in 1725. It would therefore have been played on one of the keyboard instruments in the Bach household, either on a clavichord or harpsichord (it was only later in the century that the piano became the 'normal' domestic keyboard instrument). On your audio-cassette it is played on a harpsichord – but find the piece in the Scores booklet and read on before you listen to it.

The piece is a polonaise – one of a number of dances that were popular in the eighteenth century. In addition to the notes themselves it also includes four other signs above the notes which may be new to you at this stage of the course: tr, w, w and . These 'ornaments' are a particular feature of seventeenth- and eighteenth-century music (though they were used at other times too) and are explained in numerous sources of the period. The four used in this piece have the meanings shown in Example 2.

Example 2

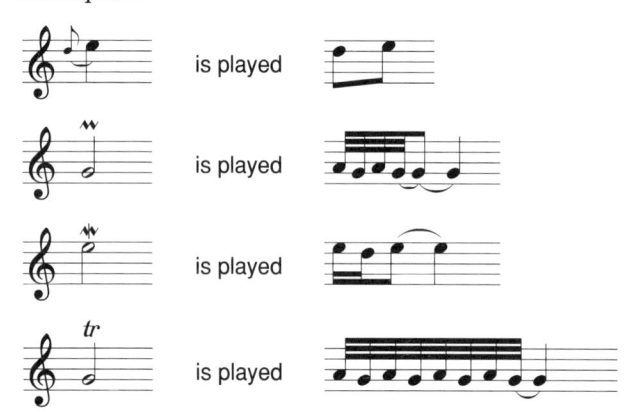

These, and other ornaments, will be studied in more detail in Unit 17. Ornaments were not written out in full in the score because they are 'ornamental', as their names suggest, and do not generally have fixed rhythmic values (the rhythmic values given above are only approximate); they vary in performance depending on factors such as the speed of the piece and the context in which they occur.

You should by now be familiar with the repeat sign at the end of bar 8, :||:, and at the end of the piece, :||. You have already met it in Unit 4, and it will be referred to again a number of times in the course. It means that the Polonaise should be performed as follows: bars 1–8 (then repeated); bars 9–28 (then repeated).

Figure 1 Clavichord, made by Hieronymous Albrecht Hass, Hamburg 1743.

Figure 2 Detail of clavichord in Figure 1. Each key forms the front arm of a lever. Depressing a key lifts the back arm, seesaw fashion. The back arm carries a metal blade (or tangent) which strikes the string and makes it vibrate. The sound is quiet, but firm playing gives a louder sound than gentle playing.

Figure 3 Harpsichord by Alan Gotto (1992) after Mietke (c.1720).

Figure 4 Detail of the harpsichord in Figure 3. Depressing a key causes a wooden 'jack' to rise (one jack is shown raised). A small plectrum projects horizontally from each jack, just visible on the raised jack. As the jack rises, the plectrum plucks the string. Releasing the key lowers the jack, and a pivot allows the plectrum to slip silently over the string. Firmness of playing does not affect the loudness of the note. (A harpsichord mechanism is shown in the video section for this unit.)

Turn again to the score of the Polonaise (Scores 2). It is longer and more complex than Example 1, so we'll deal with it in two parts, beginning with bars 1–8. We are going to try to identify the landmarks. In addition to changes in rhythm and pitch that you considered in the earlier example, it will be useful to include other features such as the number of notes played by each hand and the type of musical material used at any particular moment.

Exercise

How would you describe the musical material of bars 1 and 2?

My answer

The first two bars are mostly made up of three-note chords. In bar 1 these chords each last for a crotchet. In bar 2 this crotchet rhythm continues in the left-hand, with a more ornate right-hand part.

Exercise

How does the material of bars 3 and 4 differ from that of bars 1 and 2 (right hand especially)?

My answer

The right-hand part has a livelier rhythm.

Exercise

Characterize the type of material used in bars 5 and 6, and bars 7 and 8.

My answer

Both hands plays the same music an octave apart in bars 5 and 6. In bars 7 and 8 it is again the right hand that is most active, with a sudden upwards leap followed by a downwards scale.

Don't worry if you described this material differently from me, but make sure you have understood my descriptions before going on.

Now mark up the first 8 bars of your score, using whatever symbols are clearest to remind you of the 'events' in the music that you have just observed. My marked-up version is in Example 3.

Example 3

Listen to the first eight bars of the Polonaise, following the music in your score. These bars are recorded as audio-cassette Item 4. You should listen to this section two or three times before going on.

LISTEN TO ITEM 4 WHILE FOLLOWING THE SCORE.

Exercise

Now go through the whole of the Polonaise, making similar markings in the score. The piece has a regular phrase pattern which divides it into a series of two-bar sections. Make sure you have something marked for each of these (some of which are similar to earlier sections) and compare your markings with my answer.

My answer

In the list below, the numbers at the start of each line are bar numbers.

1, 2   Mostly chords; left hand stays on the same note.

3, 4   A more lively rhythm, especially in the right hand.

5, 6	Both hands play the same music an octave apart.
7, 8	At the beginning of bar 7 there is a sudden leap up to a high G, followed by a downward scale.
9, 10	Similar to bars 1, 2.
11, 12	Fast-moving right hand against steady left hand – until the second beat of bar 12.
13, 14	Similar to bars 5, 6.
15, 16	Similar to bars 7, 8.
17, 18	A mixture of chords (bar 17) and faster notes (bar 18).
19, 20	Exactly the same as bars 17 and 18, but down a step .
21, 22	Mostly chords; left hand stays on the same note and bar 22 repeats bar 21 exactly.
23, 24	Faster-moving right hand against a steady left hand (bar 24 is similar to bars 12, 18 and 20).
25, 26	Exactly as bars 5, 6.
27, 28	Exactly as bars 7, 8.

Now listen to audio-cassette Item 5, which is a recording of the whole Polonaise. Don't worry if you can't follow each note as it is played, but it is important that you match the main 'events' on the page with what you hear. Repeat this part of the exercise until you feel able to follow the score with a degree of confidence (remember that the piece is in two sections, each repeated).

LISTEN TO ITEM 5 AND FOLLOW THE SCORE.

2.3 ARPEGGIOS AND BROKEN CHORDS

Two very common patterns of notes, which you will meet frequently in the course and which are useful landmarks if you can spot them, are the **arpeggio** and the **broken chord**. They occur frequently, though not exclusively, in keyboard music, and you will need to remember these terms. In both cases, the notes of a chord are sounded in succession, rather than simultaneously. In arpeggios, the notes of a chord are sounded in ascending or descending order, whereas in broken chords, the notes may be sounded in any order. An example of each should clarify these terms.

Look first at the G major Polonaise of J. S. Bach, in Scores 2. In the left-hand part of bar 4, on beats 2 and 3 the last four notes of the bar all belong to the chord of D major. Since they are sounded in succession, we call this an arpeggio of D major.

Now look at the Scherzo movement from Beethoven's Piano Sonata in A major, Op. 2 No. 2, also in Scores 2 (p. 20). The first five notes of this piece all belong to the chord of A major. They are sounded one after the other, but not in the order (ascending or descending) in which they occur in that chord. This is therefore a broken chord of A major. In fact, you can see that the first 15 notes in the right hand are a broken chord of A major.

2.4 OPTIONAL EXERCISE

If you would like a little more practice before going on, you could work through another piece, the Polonaise in G minor (Scores 2, page 10), in a similar way to that of Section 2.2. It is another of the pieces from the Anna Magdalena Notebook, possibly composed by J. S. Bach's son Carl Philipp Emanuel Bach (1714–88). Before you listen to it you might like to put my suggested markings in your score.

LOOK AT THE G MINOR POLONAISE.

SUGGESTED MARKINGS

Passages where the right and left hands are in octaves (bars 1, 2, 5, 6, 9, 10, 21, 22).

Right hand in thirds, left-hand single notes (bars 3, 4, 7, 11, 12, 13, 14, 15, 23).

Left-hand groups of semiquavers (bars 4, 12, 16).

Make sure that you have noticed the repeat signs.

The first eight bars only are recorded as audio-cassette Item 6, and the whole piece as Item 7.

LISTEN TO ITEMS 6 AND 7 AND FOLLOW THE SCORE.

3 KEYBOARD SCORES II: TEXTURE AND DYNAMICS

By now you will have realised that there are several elements in a score that can act as 'pointers' or 'landmarks' to the reader: changes in rhythm, pitch, etc. The events that you follow will vary from piece to piece, depending on a number of factors such as differences in musical style, instrumentation, etc. But one of the most important elements to watch for is *texture*.

Texture concerns the density and range of the sounds that are employed. We can talk about 'high' or 'low' textures (according to whether the notes are predominantly high or low in pitch), 'thin' or 'dense' textures (according to whether there are few or many notes) or 'widely-spaced' textures (if the music has both high and low pitches and not much in the middle). In fact, you already have some experience of different textures. If you look back to the G major Polonaise you will remember that it began with 2 bars of chords (apart from the slight embellishment of the top part at the beginning of bar 2). Bars 3 and 4 of the same piece, however, had just one note at a time in each hand, apart from the chord on the first beat of bar 3. We can therefore talk of this Polonaise having a predominantly chordal texture for the first two bars, followed by a two-part texture for bars 3 and 4.

Examples 4(a), (b) and (c) contain three examples of different keyboard textures. They are recorded as audio-cassette Item 8. Listen to them, following the examples at the same time, before you read on. The arrows over the examples show where the recorded extracts begin and end.

LISTEN TO ITEM 8 AND FOLLOW EXAMPLES 4 (a), (b) AND (c).

I would describe Example 4(a) as a rather thick and quite low chordal texture. Example 4(b), on the other hand, is thin and widely-spaced. (It was played on an early piano, rather than a modern grand piano.) Example 4(c) is different again. Here, although the music is played by two hands, there are six independent strands, or 'parts' in the music, in this case three in each hand. This is certainly a complex texture; but we can go a little further, because there is a technical term for this sort of writing: this is **counterpoint**. The texture here can therefore be described as **contrapuntal**. Some pieces rely on this sort of texture throughout, such as fugues and ricercars, which were particularly popular in the sixteenth, seventeenth and eighteenth centuries – but more of this later in the course. There are many varieties of keyboard texture, and for the moment you simply need to be aware of this fact.

Example 4 contained some additional markings such as *ff* and this sign:

in the Chopin and *f* and *sf* in the Beethoven. You have encountered some of these already in Unit 3, and as a group of performance directions they are referred to as **dynamics**. They are concerned with the relative loudness or softness of performance. Dynamics were written in music as early as the seventeenth century, but came into their own after about 1750, when they began to be used with increasing frequency in scores. Most of the dynamic markings that you will encounter are either abbreviations or complete Italian words. Table 1 gives the most important ones; these and others are included in the reference material at the end of this pair of units.

Table 1

Abbreviation	Full form	Meaning
pp	pianissimo	very soft
p	piano	soft
mp	mezzo piano	moderately soft
mf	mezzo forte	moderately loud
f	forte	loud
ff	fortissimo	very loud
sf or sfz	sforzando	suddenly louder on specific notes
cresc.	crescendo	getting louder
dim.	diminuendo	getting quieter

In addition, some signs are used. You met the following two in Unit 3:

means the same as *crescendo*.

means the same as *diminuendo*.

All of these terms are printed at the back of this booklet for reference.

Dynamic contrasts are often used to reinforce the effects of texture changes. So, for example, a passage with a full texture may be played loudly to contrast with a quiet, thinner texture, or a crescendo might accompany an increasingly dense texture to form a climax in the music. Concentrating on the texture and dynamics of a piece of music can be a very useful way of following some scores.

Before we go on I would like to make one more point about Example 4(b) which has very little to do with score reading, but I hope you will find it interesting nonetheless. The recording that you listened to was made on an early piano, similar to the sort of instrument that Beethoven would have

Example 4(a) Chopin, Prélude in C minor, bars 1–4

Example 4(b) Beethoven, Sonata in C Op. 53 'Waldstein', first movement, bars 149–56

Example 4(c) J. S. Bach, Ricercar in six parts from the Musical Offering, bars 166–80

played in Vienna around the year 1800 (the extract you heard was composed in 1803/4). It sounds quite different from a modern grand piano. The same extract appears again as audio-cassette Item 9(a), and is followed immediately by a performance of the same passage on a modern grand piano, Item 9(b). Before you listen to them, I should also add that the two instruments on the recording are tuned at different pitches. Over the centuries, pitch has changed, so that early instruments rarely play at the same pitch as their modern counterparts.

LISTEN NOW TO ITEMS 9(a) AND 9(b).

The Scores 2 booklet contains the Scherzo (an Italian word meaning 'joke') and Trio from Beethoven's Piano Sonata in A major, Op. 2 No. 2, composed in 1795[1]. Like so much of Beethoven's music it is full of dramatic contrasts of texture and dynamics. Please find the score (p.20). Here is a list of the different textures used in the movement.

- Semiquavers in the right hand, chords in the left hand.
- Semiquavers in the left hand, chords in the right hand.
- Crotchet chords.
- Longer chords.
- Melody in the right hand with left-hand quaver accompaniment.

Exercise

Go through the score of the Scherzo (not the Trio yet) marking where the different textures above occur. You might like to mark the five different textures in my list with five different colours (if you have anything suitable to hand to do it with). Note also the changes in dynamics (perhaps by putting a ring around the relevant markings) and the repeat signs. In this particular movement you will probably find that the changes in texture are more helpful to you when you are listening and following the score than the dynamics.

My answer

Before you listen to the Scherzo you may like to check that you have marked the five textures that I listed in the right places. Here are my solutions (bar 1 is counted as the first full bar and bar 4^3 means 'bar 4 beat 3' – a shorthand notation which will be used from now on in the course):

Semiquavers in the right hand, chords in the left hand: bars 1, 2, 4^3–6, 32–34, 36^3–38.

Semiquavers in the left hand, chords in the right hand: bars 8^3–10, 12^3–14, 40^3–42.

Crotchet chords: bars 3, 4, 7, 8, 11, 12, 15–18, 35, 36, 39, 40, 43, 44.

Longer chords: bars 25–30.

Melody in the right hand with left-hand quaver accompaniment: bars 19–24.

In addition to these 'events' there is also a whole bar's rest in bar 31 – perhaps the biggest 'landmark' of all – and a trill in bar 22 that might help you.

As you worked through the score you may have noticed some Italian terms. Their meanings are:

Allegretto	moderately fast
rallent (short for *rallentando*)	getting slower
a tempo	back to the original speed
Fine	the end (see below)

You will find a more complete list of Italian terms and their meanings at the end of this pair of units.

Listen to the Scherzo a few times, following it in your score. It is recorded as audio-cassette Item 10. Set your counter reading to zero before you begin.

LISTEN NOW TO ITEM 10. FOLLOW IT IN THE SCORE.

Now turn to the Trio in the same score. Although this looks like a separate piece, it was in fact customary to perform a Trio after a Scherzo and then to repeat the Scherzo (stopping at the term '*Fine*' at the end of the Scherzo). The overall form for the whole movement is therefore Scherzo–Trio–Scherzo (similar to many Minuet–Trio–Minuet forms of the eighteenth century which you will meet later in the course). This is a so-called **ternary** form, because it is divided into three clearly-defined sections. You will be returning to ternary forms in Unit 10.

As I hope you will see, there is not so much contrast in the texture of the Trio as there was in the Scherzo. There are, however, several *sf* indications above,

---

[1] 'Op' is short for 'opus' the Latin term for 'work'. Composers often give 'opus' numbers to complete works, or collections of pieces.

between and below the staves. These **sforzando** indications (as you can see from Table 1) mean that the performer is instructed to emphasize, or accentuate, those particular chords. This should help you to follow the score. Notice also the crescendo marking in bars 58–60 as well as the gradual progression from *piano* to *fortissimo* in bars 61–8 (the direction *fp* in bar 61 means *forte* followed immediately by *piano*).

Listen to the Trio a few times now (remember the repeats!).

LISTEN NOW TO ITEM 11 WHILE FOLLOWING THE SCORE.

Finally, listen through to the whole movement (Scherzo–Trio–Scherzo) following the music in your score.

LISTEN NOW TO ITEM 12 WHILE FOLLOWING THE SCORE.

4 LARGER SCORES

4.1 THE ORCHESTRA

So far, all the examples you have studied in this unit have been played on either the piano or harpsichord. Our aim, however, is to help you eventually to follow an orchestral score. This means that you will need to become familiar with the characteristics and sounds of a number of instruments – but not all of them immediately! This unit will serve as an introduction: later units will fill in details as well as giving you an opportunity for more listening.

If you have watched modern symphony orchestras play you may have noticed that the performers tend to be arranged on the platform according to the 'families' to which their instruments belong (see Figures 5(a) and 5(b)).

Figure 5(a)   The London Philharmonic Orchestra with Music Director Franz Welser-Möst.

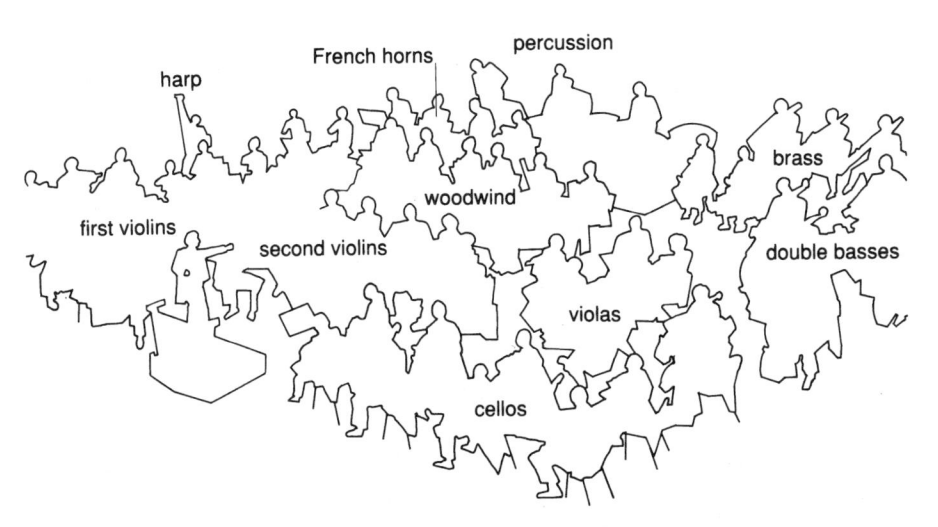

Figure 5(b)   Families of instruments in Figure 5(a).

Each family is a group of instruments sharing certain features – the way they are played and the materials of which they are made. Table 2 is a summary of the instruments most commonly used in orchestras.

Table 2 Some standard orchestral instruments

Family	English names	Italian names	Italian abbreviations
Woodwind	flutes	flauti	fl
	oboes	oboi	ob
	clarinets	clarinetti	cl
	bassoons	fagotti	fg
Brass	horns	corni	cor
	trumpets	trombe	tr
	trombones	tromboni	tbni
Percussion	kettledrums (cymbals, triangle, etc.)	timpani	timp
Strings	violins	violini	vl
	violas	viola	vla
	cellos	violoncelli	vc
	double basses	contra bassi	cb

This list will be repeated and extended in Unit 20.

Since many of the terms used in scores are Italian, it is important that you begin to familiarize yourself with some of them, and for that reason the list above includes Italian names as well as English. In most cases, the two languages have words which are similar, but there are some significant differences, especially for the double basses, bassoons, horns and drums. There are also some potential confusions: 'trombe' means trumpets, not trombones! You should also be aware that scores sometimes include singular, rather than plural terms (such as 'violino' instead of 'violini'), and slightly different abbreviations ('vln' or 'vn' rather than 'vl').

Look now at Example 5. It is the beginning of the last movement of Beethoven's Fifth Symphony as it appears in one edition. Identify the instruments used in it from Table 2.

Example 5

There are two instruments in Example 5 that I have not included in the table, but which you may nevertheless recognize. They were not included in my table because they are less 'standard' than the other members of the orchestra I mentioned, although they are quite often used in scores of the nineteenth and twentieth centuries. The first is the 'piccolo' (short for 'flauto piccolo', meaning 'small flute'), a version of the flute which plays an octave higher than the standard instrument. The other is the 'Contrafagotto' ('double bassoon' or 'contrabassoon'), a large version of the bassoon which plays an octave lower than the standard instrument. There are also some qualifying terms, such as 'Alto', 'Tenore' and 'Basso' for the trombones, which refer to different sizes (and therefore pitches) of instruments. The clarinets, horns, trumpets and drums are 'in C', but I don't propose to explain this now – you will have to wait until Unit 21.

You should also be aware that the double basses (like the double bassoon) sound an octave lower than their written pitch – a point that will be taken up later in the course.

Exercise

Now go down the score and group the instruments according to their families. Do this by bracketing the instruments together on the score and labelling them.

THIS EXTRACT IS RECORDED AS ITEM 13.

Answer and discussion

My marked-up score is given as Example 6.

Notice that the instruments in the score are arranged in 'families' according to pitch, the highest of each family being placed at the top, with the exception of the horns. Because of the way they are used in the orchestra the horns are usually placed between the woodwind and the rest of the brass.

Historically, music for more than just a handful of instruments playing at the same time began to be performed with increasing frequency in the sixteenth century, corresponding with the emergence of the violin family (the 'string' family in the table above) in northern Italy. By the end of the seventeenth century the word 'orchestra' would normally have meant 'string

Example 6

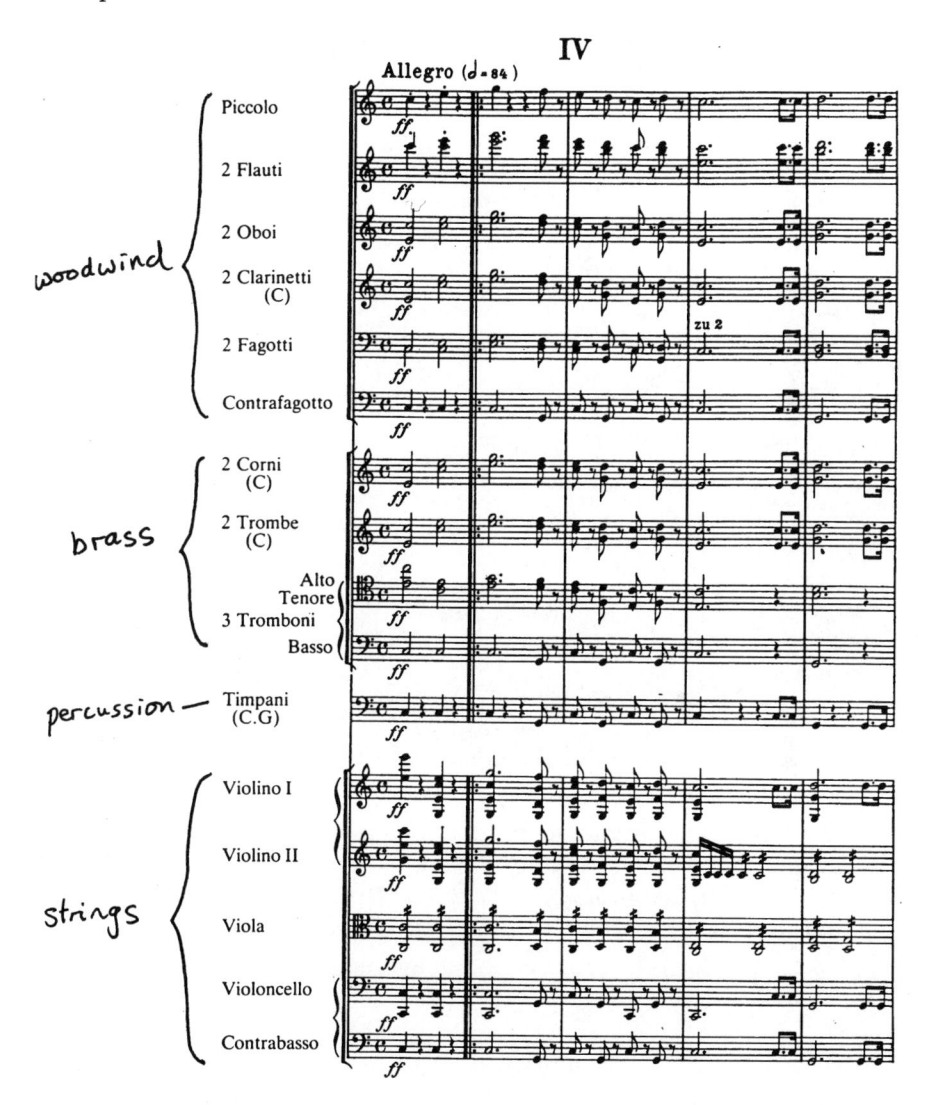

Figure 6 Horn (sometimes called the French horn). The modern instrument has valves, first introduced in the nineteenth century. These effectively alter the length of tubing, changing the fundamental note and its associated harmonic series of notes. Earlier instruments were of fixed length, or could have extra sections of tube inserted by hand.

Example 7

CONCERTO IV.

orchestra', with perhaps the addition of one or two woodwind or brass instruments. The score of Corelli's Concerto Op. 6 No. 4 is typical of orchestral music of its period (Example 7). It uses strings only, most of whom play together in the main 'band' (called the **concerto grosso** here, but sometimes **ripieno**), but with the addition of a small solo group (called the **concertino**), in this case, also strings.

Figure 7 Trumpet. Like the horn, the modern instrument has valves to alter the length of tubing. Earlier instruments were of fixed length, or could have extra sections of tube inserted.

Figure 8 The string family. From left to right: violin, viola (larger than a violin and pitched a fifth lower), cello (an octave below the viola) and double bass. All have four strings; double-basses occasionally have five. All have adjacent strings tuned a fifth apart, except for the double bass; double basses are tuned in fourths. These instruments are early nineteenth-century designs. Note the lack of a spike on the cello (for a modern cello, see Unit 2, p. 34).

During the eighteenth century, woodwind and brass instruments became an increasingly standard part of the orchestra. By the end of the eighteenth century (in the mature works of Haydn and Mozart) the 'standard' orchestra comprised the following (though there are many deviations from the 'standard'):

woodwind: 2 each of flutes, oboes, clarinets, bassoons;

brass: 2 horns, 2 trumpets;

percussion: 2 timpani (1 player);

strings: several violins (divided into first and second groups), some violas, cellos and double basses.

During the nineteenth century, more brass instruments were introduced into the orchestra. Trombones were often used by Beethoven's time (from the beginning of the century, though they had been used on occasion before) and the number of horns increased until eight were sometimes used by the end of the century. The use of percussion also grew in the nineteenth century and has been a particular feature of some twentieth-century music.

This, then, is how the modern orchestra evolved. For the moment, though, you will be listening to only a few of these instruments, but I hope you found it interesting, nevertheless, to see how individual members of the orchestra fit into a broader pattern.

Figure 9 Timpani. The only tuneable drums in the orchestra. A set of timpani comprises variously sized drums.

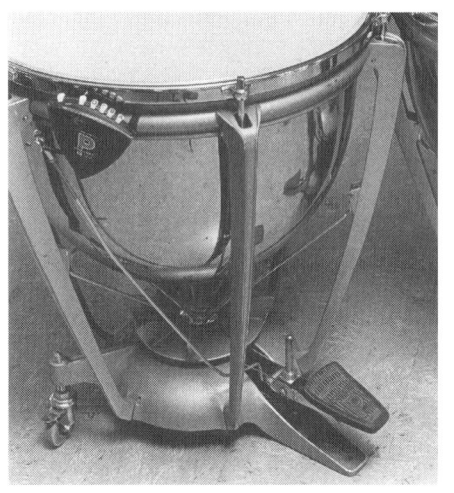

Figure 10 Modern timpani are tuned by depressing or releasing a pedal; their pitch is continuously variable over a range of about a fifth. Earlier instruments were tuned manually by turning screws around the rim.

Figure 11 A lute. The strings are arranged in closely spaced pairs, called courses. Strings in a course may be in unison, or tuned an octave apart. The player plucks a course in a single stroke, as though plucking a single string. Pitch is varied by stopping courses against transverse ridges, called frets, on the neck (as in the viol family, but unlike the violin family).

Figure 12 A theorbo. Related to the lute, but with extra bass courses and different tuning systems. Often used as a continuo instrument in the 18th century, and also as a solo instrument.

4.2 INTRODUCING FIGURED BASS AND THE CONTINUO

The rest of this unit will examine scores from the seventeenth and eighteenth centuries. A common feature of almost all music of this period for more than one instrument is the presence of a keyboard instrument, or plucked string instrument such as the lute. This was normally required to play chords above the bass line (which was usually also played by one or more cellists or bassoonists and perhaps a double bass as well). In church, the organ was most likely to be used, whereas in the opera house, concert room or in the home a harpsichord or lute would have been more usual. Towards the end of the eighteenth century, the early piano was sometimes employed. The instrument would not necessarily be mentioned in the score, however, and there would be no two-stave keyboard part for the performer to follow.

Instead, the performer of this part was expected to follow the bass part which had figures written above or below it – the **figured bass**. In Example 7 there is only one such figure (the '6' under the second bar of the 'basso' part) but you can see a much more comprehensively figured bass part in J. S. Bach's Sonata for flute and continuo in Scores 2, p.12.

📖 LOOK AT THE FIGURING IN THIS SCORE.

The figures are written below the bass stave. These figures were a shorthand, indicating to the performer which chords should be played. Bach, therefore, did not need to write out these chords in full, but a modern editor has supplied them here in the right-hand keyboard part for ease of modern performance.

Instead of just one type of instrument playing from the bass line, there would usually have been two, and perhaps more. The group of performers was called the *continuo* group, and *continuo* was the name frequently given to the bass part in scores of the period.

Now turn to Video Section 1 for a more detailed explanation of the continuo. You will need to be able to play your keyboard while watching.

4.3 THE CONTINUO

V   **VIDEO NOTES**
UNIT 9, VIDEO SECTION 1

Introduction

The object of this section of video is *not* to teach you to play a continuo part, but to familiarize you with its notation. Some of the information is rather more detailed than you need for the present, and you are not expected to master all of it now. You will probably need to refer back to it, though, as you work through the course.

🎹 NOW WATCH THE VIDEO SECTION. YOU WILL NEED YOUR KEYBOARD.

During the video

There are two points at which you will be asked to work out some chords on your keyboard. The answers to these exercises are given below.

First exercise

Video Example 1

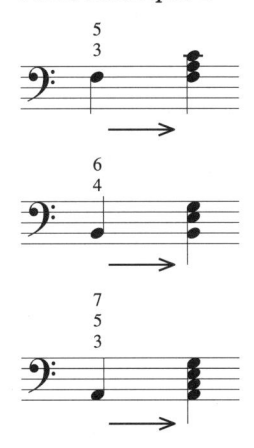

Second exercise

Video Example 2

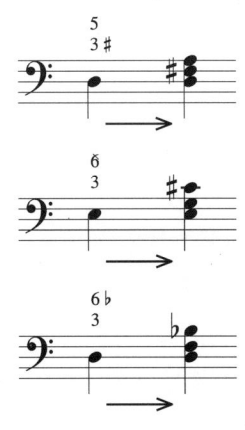

Summary

The harpischord used in the video section is a copy by Alan Gotto of an instrument made in Berlin by Mietke (*c*.1710).

Almost all vocal, chamber or orchestral music between the years 1600 and 1800 was written with a chord-playing instrument in mind – a lute, harpsichord, organ, or later, a piano. These instruments are not generally named in the score, but they were played from the bass part which had figures written above or beneath denoting the harmony to be played (see Example 7 and the Bach Sonata for flute and continuo in Scores 2).

The bass part would also be played by a cellist, double-bass player, or bassoonist (or a combination of a number of these instrumentalists) and the whole group was called the continuo group (and the part that they played, the continuo or figured bass part).

The figures above or beneath a note tell the performer the intervals of the notes to be played above the bass part. A bass note with 3 and 6 above or beneath it instructs the performer to play notes a third and a sixth above the bass note.

Video Example 3

Video Example 4

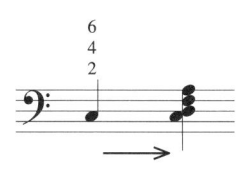

The notes of the chords are always assumed to be within the key of the piece. So if a B♭ is in the key signature, the performer will use it in a chord:

Video Example 5

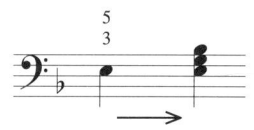

If the composer wishes to move outside of the key, the figure can be amended:

Video Example 6

Several adaptations of the figures can be used:

6̸   4+   5♯   3♮   *for sharps or naturals*

                              4♭   *for flats*

Flat, sharp and natural signs may be placed either before or after the figure they refer to.

In practice, a performer may duplicate notes of a chord, or transfer them to another register of the instrument. So a

5
3♯

over a D could be played in a number of ways:

Video Example 7

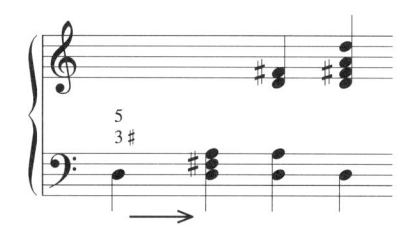

In actual continuo parts not all of the notes will be figured, such as the beginning of Corelli's Concerto Grosso in D, Op. 6 No. 4.

Video Example 8

[musical notation]

If a bass note had no figure under or over it, it was assumed that the performer would simply play a root position chord within the key signature. So, for example, the first two chords of Video Example 8 would be D major followed by B minor.

Other abbreviations are used within the system. A few more commonly used chords are often indicated by just one of their figures. So in bar 2 of Video Example 8 the '6' would be assumed to mean

6
3

a first-inversion chord.

If the bass line contains notes of faster duration than the beat, not all of these notes need to be harmonized.

Video Example 9

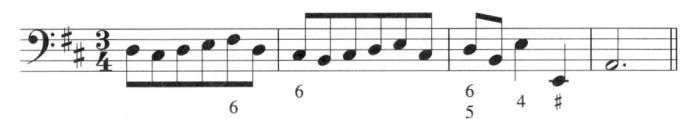

[musical notation]

In Video Example 9, for example, the continuo player would know from experience that the harmony is unlikely to change on every quaver, and would probably assume that harmony was needed only on those quavers which were on the beat, or even less frequently. Video Example 9 might therefore be played in a number of ways, two of which appear as Video Examples 10 and 11.

Video Example 10

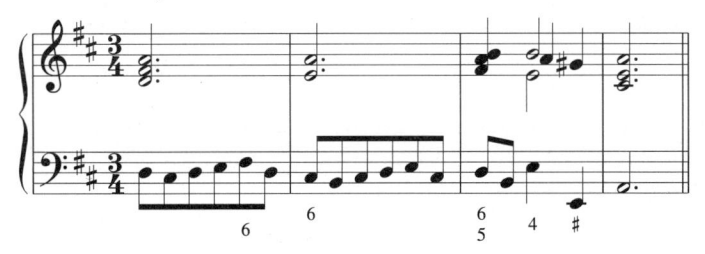

[musical notation]

Video Example 11

[musical notation]

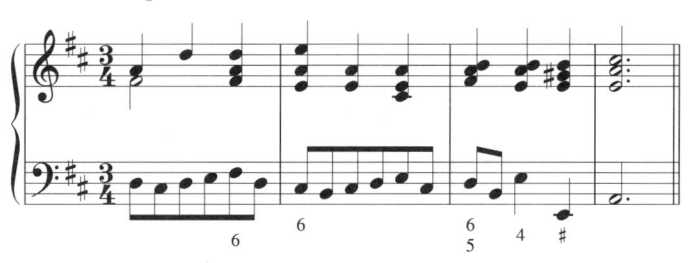

If the continuo player wanted to play in a more florid manner, with some additional notes for interest, he or she could do so, provided that the elaborations did not interfere with the rest of the music. Video Example 12 shows a typical example.

Video Example 12

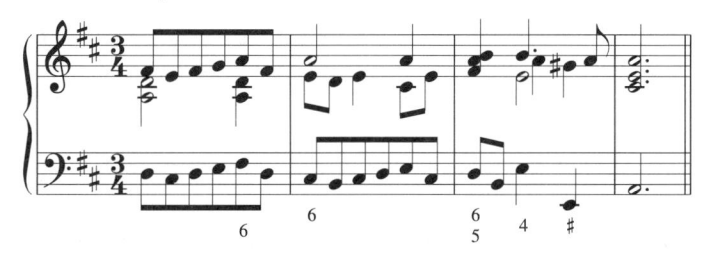

[musical notation]

A great deal of choice lies with the performer in continuo parts, so that no two performances of the same piece are likely to contain exactly the same notes.

5 SOLO SONATAS WITH CONTINUO

Exercise

Scores 2 contains the third movement of the Sonata Op. 5 No. 1 for violin and continuo by Arcangelo Corelli (1653–1713) (p.26). Look at bars 1–9 and make a list of the significant musical features of the extract that might help you to follow the score.

Discussion

The following seem to me to be important things to note:

1   The groups of short notes placed under slurs in the violin part in bars 2 and 6 (and to a lesser extent in bar 8). These are ornamental notes that are meant to sound as if they have been improvised 'on the spot' – more of this in a moment. You may notice that the note values in these bars do not add up to the number of beats that they ought to. In bar 2, for example, there are strictly speaking four minims' worth of notes, rather than the three that there should be. This is because the notation is following a convention found in some music whereby very short notes are not notated in a rhythmically strict way. That is all you need to know about this sort of notation now – it is rarely used, and you won't have to write anything in this notation during the course. What is important here is that you have registered the presence of some groups of notes that will be played much faster than others – a very useful visual 'landmark'. (Incidentally, its also a useful illustration of the fact that scores with more notes in them are not necessarily more difficult to follow than those with fewer – in this case, the contrast of passages of long notes with those of short notes will probably make following the score more manageable.)

2   There are two important moments when the violin part is less active: at the imperfect cadences in bars 5 and 9. In both places the violin has long notes followed by rests.

3   The rise and fall of the violin line.

In comparison with the violin part, the continuo line is relatively uninteresting, and when you listen to the piece most of your attention will probably be focused on the top stave, although you may find the slow, measured progress of the bass line in minims and semibreves easier to follow than the violin in places.

You may like to mark these features in your score. Alternatively, this might be a good point at which to try following the score as it stands, having taken note of the important features of the music.

Listen to the first nine bars of this piece, following them in your score. They are recorded as audio-cassette Item 14. Don't try to hear all of the individual notes in the violin part – the ornamented passages go so quickly that it is better just to register each of them in your mind as a group of fast notes. Remember also that you will be hearing three instruments, not two. The continuo part is played by the cello and organ. As you may know, the word *Adagio* at the beginning indicates that the movement is to be played slowly. One or two additional notes are played by the performers on this recording; but this should not hinder your score reading.

LISTEN TO ITEM 14 WHILE FOLLOWING THE SCORE.

Listen to item 14 several times, if necessary, until you are confident that you can follow the short extract, then do the following exercise.

Exercise

In the remainder of the score mark in events similar to those I pointed out in the first nine bars. Compare your working with my answer before you listen to the extract.

Answer

The numbers on the left below are bar numbers.

14   A rest in the violin part.

14–17 The bass line plays only on the first and second beats of the bar.

18–19 The violin part rises to a climax and then falls quickly.

20   The bass line rests.

24   The violin is very low in its register.

29   A cadence followed by a long note in the violin part.

32–4   More rests in the violin part.

40–1   Two long groups of fast notes in the violin part in quick succession.

Now listen to the complete movement, following it in your score. It is recorded as audio-cassette Item 15. Set your counter reading to zero and repeat the exercise a few times.

LISTEN TO ITEM 15 WHILE FOLLOWING THE SCORE.

The sonata you have been studying first appeared in 1710, ten years after Corelli had published the piece in a simpler version. Nine bars of this earlier, simpler version appear in Example 8.

Example 8

If you compare the violin parts of Example 8 and the later version in Scores 2 (p. 26) you will see that the later version (in Scores 2) has many more notes in the violin part than Example 8. This is explained on the title page of the edition from which the version in Scores 2 is taken, which claims that the added ornaments represent the way in which Corelli himself performed the music. Whether or not Corelli did actually play the piece exactly like this is uncertain – publishers were not above making such claims for purely commercial reasons, so it is impossible to be sure. It is known, however, that instrumentalists and singers at the time frequently ornamented simple melodic lines (especially in slow pieces) so that the resulting performance was much more ornate than the score itself would suggest. This practice of improvised ornamentation has been revived, so you may from time to time come across performances that don't quite match the corresponding scores.

The next piece we are going to look at is from another sonata, this time for flute and continuo. It is by J. S. Bach and is recorded as audio-cassette Item 16. The score is reproduced in Scores 2, p.12.

You saw part of a score of this piece in the video section for this unit. The score in the video section differs from the one in Scores 2: on the video recording, there is a single stave for the continuo, whereas in Scores 2 the continuo part has two staves (right and left hand for the keyboard player). What Bach actually wrote was the version on the video recording. From the single-stave continuo part with figures, Bach expected the keyboard player to improvise music for both hands based on harmony indicated by the figures. As I mentioned in Section 4.2, the editor of the version reproduced in Scores 2 has written out a right-hand keyboard part to help the modern performer. It does not exactly correspond to what you hear on the audio-cassette (because the performer on the recording has chosen to 'realise' the part in a different way), but it is a good example of the sort of accompaniment a performer might play. *In the following discussion, when I use the word 'continuo' I am referring just to the left hand part of the continuo in the scores booklet.*

A quick glance through the piece will be sufficient to show you that there are going to be no dramatic changes in texture and dynamics, and that there are several passages where the rhythmic patterns change little from bar to bar – the flute part has many long stretches of continuous semiquavers, and the continuo part moves mainly in quavers.

Exercise

What landmarks are there to help in following the score?

My answer

A number of 'events' come to mind:

(a) Occasional long notes in the flute part (e.g. bar 5).

(b) Passages where the bass part has semiquavers instead of quavers (e.g. bars 5, 11–13).

(c) A rhythmic pattern in the continuo part (bars 17, 18) where the crotchets start off the beat rather than on the beat.

(d) Occasional rests, mainly in the bass (e.g. bars 9, 10).

(e) Important cadences (bars 9 and 17).

The direction at the beginning of the piece, 'Adagio ma non tanto' is rather a complex one, meaning 'slowly, but not too much so'.

Identify some of these events (try to avoid marking them) and then listen to the movement (twice if you found it difficult first time), following it in your score.

> LISTEN TO ITEM 16 WHILE FOLLOWING THE SCORE.

How did following this score compare with your experience of following the Corelli sonata movement? You probably had to pay more attention to the continuo part in the Bach example than the Corelli. This is simply because the continuo part is more interesting in Bach's piece – it enters into more of a partnership with the top part than Corelli's does. (That is not to say that Bach's movement is any better than Corelli's; it is just a different style of piece.) As a result of this different style of writing you probably found that you had to keep dividing your attention between the two lines of music. You will find this happening more and more, especially as the number of instruments increases.

Incidentally, the rhythmic pattern in the continuo at bars 17, 18 that I referred to is an example of syncopation. The crotchets start half a beat before the second and fourth beats, and continue to sound at the instants when the beats would be expected. The effect is to make it sound as though the accents that would have fallen on beats 2 and 4 had moved forward (i.e. earlier) in the bar. The accents now appear to fall where there would normally be no accent, that is, half a beat after beat 1, and half a beat after beat 3.

> **Syncopation** is the displacement of a musical accent from a relatively strongly accented note onto a note that would normally be unaccented or only weakly accented.

You can also see and hear syncopation in bars 11, 12 and 13 of the continuo part. Notice how some notes coinciding with strong beats, such as those on beat 3 of bars 11 and 12 and beat 1 of bars 12 and 13, are not sounded on the beat, but are tied to earlier notes played off the beat. In each case the earlier note appears to take the accent from the later note.

Tying notes together is just one way of creating syncopation; other ways include using rests, and adding accent marks to normally unaccented notes.

Listen to the movement again, a number of times if necessary.

While you were working through the last two pieces you may have wondered whether there was any significance in the titles – **Sonata** in both cases. The term was used for a great number of works, especially in the period c.1650–1850. It was used earlier and later as well, and in the first place meant nothing more than that the piece was played (the Italian word 'sonata' means 'sounded' rather than sung). After about 1650, beginning in Italy, 'Sonata' came to mean a piece of music for a soloist or small group, usually in three or four distinct sections, or 'movements'. The pieces you have been listening to belong to one of the most popular manifestations of the sonata in the Baroque era: both are for solo instrument with continuo accompaniment and both have four movements.

6 TRIO SONATAS

Another very popular type of sonata was the 'Trio Sonata', so-called because the music was written on three staves, although in fact there were usually four performers (because, as we've observed, the continuo part was normally played by two instrumentalists, a 'sustaining instrument' and a chord-playing one). Corelli wrote a number of trio sonatas which were very popular in Italy and elsewhere and his style had many imitators. An important feature of trio sonata texture is the distinctive grouping of the instruments. Usually, the top two instruments are similar in pitch: Corelli used two violins, whereas other composers favoured a number of different combinations, as you will see. Because of their similarity in pitch, the two treble instruments tend to borrow musical ideas and phrases from each other, a technique that is generally called **imitation**. The stringed bass instrument is usually separated in pitch from the others and tends not to share the same musical material (although sometimes the bass part will 'borrow' a phrase or two from the top parts). The role of the other continuo player is usually to fill in the gap between the bass and the other two instruments with chords and other figuration (i.e. patterns of notes).

Scores 2 (p.29) includes a three-movement trio sonata by George Frederick Handel (1685–1759). It was written half a century or so after Corelli's trio sonatas, but it nevertheless contains all of the features described in the previous paragraph. The top two instruments (violin and oboe) are similar in pitch and they share the same musical material. The first oboe phrase of the Adagio, for example, is repeated a bar later by the violin. This pattern is reversed in bars 8 and 9 of the same movement. The same process is evident in the following Allegro movement: the oboe begins, and is 'answered' five bars later by the violin, except this time the violin's material is played a fifth higher than the oboe's, and so on through the movement. The continuo part on the other hand tends to 'plod' along rather more, with less interesting material.

Before attempting to identify the landmarks in the exercise below, you may need to familiarize yourself with the sound of the oboe and violin. In order to do so you will need to listen to the opening of this trio sonata. It begins with the continuo on its own. About two seconds later the oboe enters with a short phrase which is repeated on the violin, after which the oboe comes in again. Listen to the first 15 seconds or so of Item 17, as I've described it, without following the music in the score at first, to make sure you can differentiate between instruments. Repeat the exercise if you have any difficulty with it.

LISTEN TO THE FIRST 15 SECONDS OF ITEM 17.

Exercise

Identify some of the following landmarks in the score of the first two movements of the Handel trio sonata. (I have not supplied you with an answer, so you are on your own now.)

(a) Changes in texture: continuo alone, oboe and continuo, violin and continuo, all instruments together. These are likely to be the most helpful elements of the piece when you come to follow it in your score, especially since the sounds of the oboe and violin can easily be distinguished.

(b) Long notes.

(c) Moments in the Allegro when the bass line ceases its quaver motion.

(d) Important cadences (such as bar 7).

There are two other points to note before you listen to the recording:

- *Adagio* means 'slow', *Allegro* means 'fast' or 'lively', *Grave* (at the end of the Allegro movement) means 'very slowly'.

- The performers on your recording occasionally improvise some ornamentation that isn't in the score, but never in such a way as to interrupt the flow of the music.

Now listen to the first two movements (Adagio followed by Allegro), which are recorded as audio-cassette Items 17 and 18. Set your counter reading to zero and repeat the exercise. If you get lost, don't worry; this is a more difficult exercise than earlier ones, especially the Allegro.

LISTEN TO ITEMS 17 AND 18 WHILE FOLLOWING THE SCORE.

If you would like more practice at this point, go on to the next movement, which is another Allegro. It is in Scores 2 (p.31) and recorded as audio-cassette Item 19.

Trio sonatas form a large proportion of the chamber music repertoire of the late-seventeenth and early-eighteenth centuries, especially in Italy. The trio sonata grouping was not just important in chamber music, however. It was also the basis of a considerable amount of orchestral music of the period. Corelli's Concerto in D major, Op. 6 No. 4, demonstrates this. If you look at your score of the work (Scores 1) you will notice that the parts for the instruments are laid out as follows:

Violino I concertino (the solo first violin part)

Violino II concertino

Violoncello concertino.

Violino I Concerto Grosso (the orchestral first violin part)

Violino II Concerto Grosso

Viola Concerto Grosso

Basso Concerto Grosso

The top three staves are for the trio sonata group, in this case two violins, cello and an unmentioned continuo instrument. This is the 'solo' group which plays against the rest of the orchestra, which is represented by the bottom four staves. By using these groups of instruments separately or together the composer can create a number of different textures. This contrast of groups is one of the most important features of late baroque orchestral music, that is, orchestral music from *c*.1680 to 1750.

Turn now to the third movement of the concerto. It begins on page 7 of Scores 1 and is marked *Vivace* ('lively' – and fast). To begin with, you will be asked to follow the solo group – it is the group of three staves bracketed together at the top of the score. For the moment, disregard the other staves.

Exercise

Look through the music for this trio group for the whole of the movement identifying the following. (Again, I have not supplied an answer.)

(a) The repeat marks (the order in which the sections are performed in this movement is bars 1–8, repeat of bars 1–8, bars 9–24, repeat of bars 9–24, bars 25–27). Each section ends with a longer note.

(b) The trills in the violin parts.

(c) Rhythmic changes in the cello part – sometimes quavers, sometimes crotchets.

(d) Dynamics – remember, *p* (piano) means soft, *f* (forte) means loud.

Now listen to the movement, following the music in your score. You will hear the whole movement played by the trio group only.

LISTEN NOW TO ITEM 20 WHILE FOLLOWING THE SCORE.

When you have listened to the trio group playing the movement on their own, look at the parts of the score that we have ignored so far.

You will notice that the orchestra does not play until bar 5. When it does, the violin and cello parts play the same notes as the trio group. In the second section of the movement (beginning at bar 9), there is a similar pattern: sometimes the trio group plays alone, and sometimes it is joined by the rest of the orchestra, playing almost identical music (the differences are very small).

Now listen to audio-cassette Item 21, which is a recording of all the instruments playing this movement. Follow the music in your score, paying most attention to the trio group, but noticing where the rest of the orchestra plays, and where it is silent. Set your counter reading to zero and repeat this part of the exercise.

LISTEN NOW TO ITEM 21 AND FOLLOW THE SCORE.

Did you find following the score more or less difficult this time? More instruments playing doesn't necessarily mean that the task of following the score is more difficult. In fact, the changes in texture that the presence of the full orchestra brought about might actually have made the task of following the score easier.

LISTEN TO THE MOVEMENT A FEW MORE TIMES.

As an optional exercise you might like to go on to the next movement of Corelli's concerto to see if you can follow it in the score. You will find it recorded as Item 22.

LISTEN TO ITEM 22 AND FOLLOW THE SCORE IF YOU WISH.

7 SUMMARY

By the end of this unit you should be able to follow a keyboard score or a three-stave piece with reasonable success; not, perhaps, with ease at the first attempt but with some competence after two or three tries.

Reading a score requires the ability to spot a range of musical landmarks, and this unit has introduced you to some of the commoner ones. In particular, the following were identified, and you should be able to recognize and use them:

cadences,

dynamic marks

expression marks

instrumentation and orchestral groupings of instruments

melodic and accompanimental patterns, including arpeggios and broken chords,

ornamentation

rhythmic patterns, including syncopation,

tempo marks

You also met the concept of musical texture, and heard (and saw) the characteristic textures of the solo sonata with continuo, the trio sonata and the concerto grosso. You should also understand, in principle, how a continuo part is realized from a figured bass

Score reading, like any other musical skill, improves with practice. 'A little and often' is the best approach. You will have plenty of other opportunities to practise this skill in the course of studying other topics. Wherever possible, try to make sure that you listen to the music while following it in a score. If you would like more practice now you could go on to some of the scores used in connection with Unit 10 as a preparation for your study of that unit.

ACKNOWLEDGEMENTS

Figures 1 and 2   Bate Collection of Musical Instruments, Faculty of Music, University of Oxford.

Figure 5   Photo: Chris davies by courtesy of the London Philharmonic Orchestra Ltd.

UNIT 10

FORMAL PRINCIPLES I

Prepared for the Course Team by David Rowland

CONTENTS

1	**CONTENT AND AIMS**	30
	PART 1: VARIATION TECHNIQUES	31
2	**OSTINATO**	31
3	**THE GROUND BASS**	33
3.1	PURCELL'S GROUND IN G MAJOR	33
3.2	PURCELL'S 'AH! BELINDA'	36
4	**VARIATION FORMS**	38
	PART 2: BINARY AND TERNARY FORMS	41
5	**TERNARY FORMS**	41
6	**BINARY FORMS**	44
7	**THE SONATA PRINCIPLE**	46
8	**SUMMARY**	48

DAY 1	1	
	2	
	3-3.1	
DAY 2	3.2	
DAY 3	4	
DAY 4	5	
	6	
DAY 5	7	
	8	

All audio items for this unit can be found on Audio-cassette 4.

There are no video items for this unit.

The scores items are in Scores 2, and in your score of Purcell's *Dido and Aeneas*.

1 CONTENT AND AIMS

This unit discusses formal principles – the ways in which music is 'put together', or structured. In order to give you some idea of what a study of this involves, and to demonstrate that it is not an entirely new activity, I want you to start with a very short exercise that should take between 5 and 10 minutes.

Exercise

In Unit 4 you were given an example of plainsong to listen to. That example is reproduced here (Example 1) and is recorded as audio-cassette Item 1. Listen to it again now, asking yourself one of the questions that occurred in the earlier unit: can you hear any relationships or musical connections between the four lines of melody?

Example 1

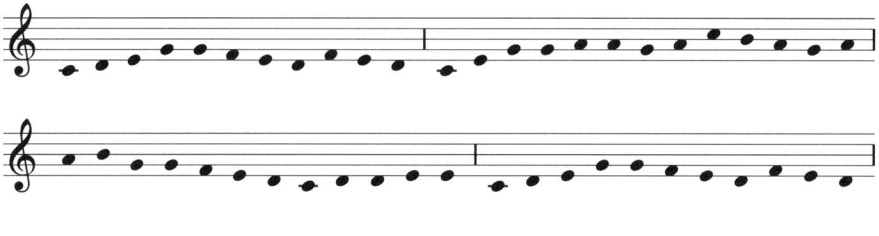

LISTEN NOW TO ITEM 1 AND FOLLOW EXAMPLE 1.

Answer

The first and fourth sections are identical while the second and third introduce new material.

I hope this was a fairly straightforward exercise. The reason for asking you to do it was in order to make some general observations about music. Three important points, it seems to me, arise from it:

1 There is structure in music, even in the simplest of works.
2 That structure can usually be recognized by asking straightforward questions such as 'can you hear any relationships or musical connections between sections of a piece?'
3 Structure is normally defined by elements of repetition and contrast.

Points 2 and 3 amount to much the same thing, underlining the fact that discovering the form of a piece of music is not a highly complex technique that takes years to learn: it is often a simple task, and one that you have already done a number of times in this course.

You may be wondering why, however, if analysing the structure of music can be so simple, two whole units are devoted to the subject 'formal principles'. The answer is straightforward. In the history of music there are hundreds of thousands of works by numerous different composers; yet only a very small number of basic formal structures are used in most of them. Studying 'formal principles' is therefore one of the most important ways of investigating Western music of the last few centuries. It provides a means of understanding how individual composers work and how music changes from one generation to the next. It also helps us to assess the skills and judgement of composers, and to understand why the music of one endures for centuries while that of another quickly becomes forgotten. In other words, an understanding of musical forms and their development is vital to our understanding of the history of Western music.

The aim of this unit is to introduce you to some of the simplest but most frequently used forms in the period c.1550–1900. In studying these forms you will be looking again at some of the works already discussed in Unit 9 as well as beginning to study one of the set works. By studying the music you will also be practising your score reading, as well as reminding yourself of some of the elements that were discussed in the first part of the course: chords, keys, etc. By the end of the unit you will be well on the way to fulfilling one of the goals of this course, which is to be able to understand the way pieces of music 'work'.

Finally, by way of introduction, I should warn you that I will be using some terminology in this unit that was introduced in Unit 6, but which you may have forgotten. In Section 5.3 of that unit all of the notes of the scale were identified with terms such as 'tonic', 'supertonic', 'mediant', etc. I will be using two of those terms in particular; 'tonic' (the first note, or degree, of the scale) and 'dominant' (the fifth note, or degree, of the scale). They will be used to identify individual notes as well as the harmony based on those notes – but I will remind you of their meaning when I use them! From now on in the course, however, you will encounter a number of these terms more frequently, so a few minutes' revision of that section of Unit 6 could be time well spent.

PART 1 VARIATION TECHNIQUES

2 OSTINATO

Of all the well-known principles of composition in Western music, and indeed music worldwide, variations have perhaps the longest history. Variations come in all shapes and sizes, but they all have one essential feature in common; a passage of music (long or short) is repeated several times. One or more elements of that passage remain constant while the composer invents other textures and patterns around them.

Probably the simplest type of variation is that in which a short melody or rhythm is repeated several times in its entirety, anywhere in the texture of a piece of music. This is called an **ostinato** (Italian for 'obstinate'). Around it, a composer is free to add music for voices or instruments, or one or more musicians may improvise (as in jazz, for example). As a method of composing it is very old – considerably older than the other variation forms you will be meeting in this unit – but it has also been taken up by a number of twentieth-century composers. Example 2 is a short passage from Ravel's (1875–1937) *Bolero*, possibly the best-known example of ostinato in the twentieth century. In this piece, the rhythm of Example 3 (overleaf) is the main recurring element.

Example 2   Opening of Ravel's Bolero

Example 3

Example 3 is played a total of 169 times on snare drum while the rest of the orchestra gradually *crescendos* towards a climax at the end. (The bass line is also repeated, but varies occasionally.) A somewhat lengthier extract is recorded on audio-cassette Item 2 so that you can hear the effect of the ostinato repetitions. Listen to this extract now.

LISTEN NOW TO ITEM 2.

The *Bolero*'s rhythmic ostinato is a very straightforward example of the technique: the repetition is exact and consistent throughout. Composers have not always kept to such a strict pattern of repetition, however. Look at Example 4.

It is an organ hymn, *Eterne rex altissime*, by John Redford (d. 1547), an early English composer for the keyboard. (An organ hymn is an organ piece based on a plainsong melody.) In this piece there is a recurring phrase which is first heard three times in the right-hand part, then in the tenor (the highest notes in the left-hand part in bars 5–6), then again in the right hand (bars 7–10), etc. Throughout the piece it occurs in different parts of the texture but does not always begin on the same note. The pattern of repetition is not consistent either: sometimes it is repeated 'end to end', as at the beginning, whereas on other occasions there is an overlap of two parts playing this figure, one starting before the other has finished, as in bars 13 and 14, or bars 16 and 17. Example 4 is recorded as audio-cassette Item 3.

LISTEN TO ITEM 3 AND FOLLOW EXAMPLE 4.

Example 4   Eterne rex altissime (*'Everlasting King in the highest'*)

As well as providing the framework for whole movements (which is relatively rare), an ostinato is used more frequently for a brief section of a movement. It is a technique that you may encounter in a number of different contexts, so it is important that you remember what the term *ostinato* means.

3 THE GROUND BASS

The **ground bass** is sometimes referred to as a type of ostinato. This is because pieces with the title 'ground bass' (or 'ground') are formed over the constant repetition of a phrase in the bass part. These pieces have two special characteristics, however, which mark them out from other ostinatos. First, the recurring element is always in the bass part (unlike the 'migrating' ostinato of Example 4), and secondly, the repeated phrases tend to be longer and more melodically interesting than many ostinati, being typically four or eight bars long.

Ground basses were particularly popular in the Baroque era (roughly 1600–1750), especially in England. (Similar but not identical forms were also used on the continent. They were often called 'Chaconne' or 'Passacaglia', titles derived from dances.) A ground normally begins with a four – or eight – bar section, beginning and ending in the tonic key, and introducing the bass line which will be repeated in successive sections of the piece. Above the bass part for this first section the composer usually writes a melody, or some other simple texture (though occasionally the bass line will be presented on its own). For the rest of the piece, it is this texture (and sometimes the speed or metre) that is varied to prevent any monotony which would otherwise result from the constant repetition of the bass line.

3.1 PURCELL'S GROUND IN G MAJOR

Scores 2 (p.52) has a Ground by Henry Purcell (1659–95) in G major. Look at it briefly, noticing the changes of texture and the different types of rhythm that are used. Then listen to it two or three times (after setting your counter reading to zero). The Ground is performed without repeats on the recording.

LISTEN TO ITEM 4 WHILE FOLLOWING THE SCORE.

Some of the notes in the score carry symbols that are probably new to you – in particular the following:

Their meanings are the same as those of the signs you came across in Unit 9; but in that instance you were studying music, and its notation, from early eighteenth-century Germany, whereas Purcell's Ground dates from late seventeenth-century England. Its notation is accordingly slightly different. The meaning of the ornament symbols and their equivalents in the music you studied in Unit 9 are as shown in Example 5.

Example 5

You will also notice in the score that there are some rhythmic values indicated in small type above the stave as well as dots and ornament signs in square brackets. All these symbols have been added by the editor of this score as suggestions for performance; not all of them were taken up in the recording in Item 4. A further editorial marking can be seen in bar 39 where the slur in the right-hand part has a vertical line through it (to distinguish it from an original slur, which would not have had the vertical line). Accidentals in parentheses (that is, in round brackets like these) have been added as cautionary accidentals; the editor has not actually changed anything, but in every case the cautionary accidental warns the performer to play a C natural rather than C♯ (which has been used on the previous beat or in the previous bar).

You should now be in a position to make some preliminary observations about this piece by answering a few questions:

Exercise

(a) How many bars long is the first statement of the bass part (before it is repeated)?

(b) Into how many sections does the piece divide?

(c) Where does the bass line deviate from the normal pattern of straightforward repetition?

Answer and discussion

The answer to (a) is that it lasts for eight bars. Example 6 contains the bass part only, as it appears in its first statement. If you did not get the right answer to this question, make sure now that you have identified this first statement correctly before you read on. You may also like to put a phrase mark over each of the eight-bar sections so that the structure of the piece is clear.

If you were right with question (a), then (b) should have been easy; the answer is eight sections in all (the first statement and seven variations). This structure has been emphasized in the score by repeat signs at the end of each section.

Question (c) is probably the most interesting because it begins to demonstrate how a composer of Purcell's stature takes liberties with the 'standard' formal procedure in order to maintain interest throughout the piece. In your answer to the question you most probably noted down bars 41–9, 60 and 62 as the places where Purcell deviates from his 'set' bass line. Yet a close examination of Example 7, which includes all the repetitions of the bass line, reveals that no two versions of it are the same. (Note: Bar 44 of Example 7 differs slightly from the corresponding bar in Scores 2. Example 7 gives the bass part as it is actually played on the audio-cassette, where an alternative reading of bar 44 from that given in Scores 2 is used.)

This raises a number of issues. First of all, if all the versions of the bass line are in fact different, what do they all have in common? The answer is that the overall melodic shape of the bass line remains essentially the same in each case – that is, the most important notes in each bar remain the same, even if there are slight changes in the rhythm. The fourth bar of each statement of the bass is the best example. Here, the note D is undoubtedly more important than any others in these bars because it is the root of the chord of D major, the harmony of that bar. This harmony is retained at the equivalent point in each repetition of the bass, yet the bass line itself appears in six different versions. All of these versions, however, emphasise the note D; it is the first note of the bar every time, and it is usually the longest as well. The effect of changing the rhythm, therefore, is not to alter the fundamental nature of the line, but simply to decorate it, thereby providing additional interest for the listener.

Taking the discussion a step further, we might ask why this bar in particular has been singled out for special treatment (no other bar is subject to the same degree of variation). The answer, I think, is twofold. First, bar 4 and its equivalents are important moments in each section because they represent the midpoint – more often than not this is also marked by the music of the upper parts coming to rest momentarily as one phrase finishes and another begins. The bass line often counteracts this lull in the momentum with more activity. Secondly, these are important moments harmonically. This piece is in the key of G major – its key signature as well as the opening and closing harmonies tell us this. If you refer back to your chord card for G major (with a tonic chord of G B D) you will see that the chord on the dominant (chord V – the root position chord formed on the fifth, or dominant, note of the scale) of G major is D major (D F♯ A). Because it is the dominant, D major is more important in the harmonic hierarchy than any other chord apart from the tonic. It is no accident, then, that our attention is particularly drawn to this bar.

One final point could be made about the different versions of the bass part. It is clear from looking at Example 7 that the most noticeably different versions of the bass line come at the end of the piece. The effect of this is to increase the momentum towards a climax just before the final cadence.

Now listen to Purcell's Ground again (following it in your score), this time taking note of the ways in which Purcell varies the rhythm and texture of the **upper parts** (i.e. everything apart from the bass line) in each section.

Example 6

Example 7

LISTEN AGAIN TO ITEM 4 AND FOLLOW THE COMPLETE SCORE

The most obvious point to make here is that Purcell varies the texture and rhythm for each repeat of the bass line – no two sections are identical. You might object at this point, claiming that the rhythm ♪♪ recurs several times in the course of the movement. You would, of course, be right in one sense, because that rhythm occurs in five out of the eight sections. But its use is different in each case. In bars 1–8 it is never used in more than one beat at a time, always on the last beat of the bar and always in the left-hand part. In bars 9–16, its use is increased, first of all to two beats at a time, and then to a complete bar. This only happens once, however (bar 14), and it is not until the next section that a more extended passage of the rhythm occurs (in bars 20–23), providing a climax not just to that section, but to the whole of the piece so far. The following section (bars 25–32) is rather more relaxed, and the texture changes. The movement here is almost entirely in crotchets, but these are shared between the hands (as a contrast to the previous sections, where most of the activity was concentrated in the right hand part). The placing of this calmer section in the middle of the work is strategic; from this point on (starting at bar 33) the momentum is increased. First, the dotted rhythm returns (now more or less continuous) in the right hand and then in the left. Then, in bars 49–56, a rather 'jagged' figure appears. This is a particularly active section, not least because there is no single melodic line to follow; the listener's attention is constantly pulled between the right and left-hand parts as they continue their syncopated rhythm. Finally, the last section brings the activity to a peak with its semiquaver scales, subsiding only just in time for the final cadence.

Listen to Purcell's Ground once or twice more, following the music in your score and noticing the effects of all these changing rhythms and textures.

LISTEN TO ITEM 4 AGAIN AND FOLLOW THE SCORE.

I hope you didn't find the previous discussion too tedious! It was necessary in order to give you some idea of how a composer can manipulate what might appear to be a boring and repetitive formal structure into a lively and interesting piece of music. If you did find the discussion difficult, return to it later, at the end of Part I. In doing so, you may also find that you have additional thoughts yourself about how the piece 'works' – a second or third look often provokes new ideas. For the moment, though, I would like to summarize some of the important features of Purcell's Ground in G major:

1. As in all grounds, the basis for the composition is the recurring bass line (in this case 8 bars long with modifications on subsequent appearances.)
2. The sections of the piece are very clearly defined.
3. Although there are eight clearly defined sections, there is a larger sense of structure which makes bars 25–32 a central, less active, part of the whole.
4. Within the self-imposed discipline of the form, Purcell has managed to create a considerable degree of variety.

Purcell's Ground in G major is just one of a number of works by him in the same form. The form appears not only in his keyboard music, but also in works for larger combinations of instruments or voices. *Dido and Aeneas* contains a number of examples, among them 'Ah! Belinda', beginning on page 6 of your score. I have chosen it for study here for two main reasons; first, it should be well within your score-reading capabilities by now, and secondly, it represents a more flexible or 'sophisticated' approach to the form than the G major Ground you have just been looking at.

3.2 PURCELL'S 'AH! BELINDA'

Find 'Ah! Belinda' in your score (p.6) and glance through it, taking no more than a minute or so. Then read on. Everything that is written in small type in your score is editorial (including the musical notes): Purcell wrote the vocal line, and figured-bass part only. The editor has 'realised' the latter for modern performance – that is, the editor has provided a worked-out version of what a keyboard player might play.

Purcell has set himself a challenge here. There is a considerable amount of text to set and the drama demands a lengthy and substantial movement at this point in the opera, but Purcell has chosen to use the ground bass form, with the bass part repeating every four bars. As we have already seen, a ground bass form of this length will need plenty of variety if it is to remain interesting. But Purcell is very restricted in the textures that he can use: the voice can only sing a single melodic line (or nothing at all) and the bass line likewise consists of one note at a time. It is possible that the keyboard con tinuo player could introduce more variety by accompanying each section differently, but the role of the keyboard is a supporting one and is unlikely to affect the piece in a fundamental way. What options, then, are open to the composer if his approach is to be a varied one?

Exercise

Set your counter reading and listen to 'Ah! Belinda' (Item 5) following the music in your score. Then do so again, this time asking the question: how has Purcell kept the music from sounding repetitious and falling into regular four-bar units? (This is quite a difficult question; don't spend too long on it before going on.)

LISTEN TO ITEM 5 AND FOLLOW YOUR SCORE.

My answer

There are at least three points, I think:

(a) The voice part does not stop at the end of each four-bar section; it often carries on, disguising rather than reinforcing the sectional nature of the music.

(b) Purcell does not always keep to a strict repetition pattern of the bass line; two of the four-bar sections start on the note G (between bars 29 and 36) rather than C – more on this below.

(c) Both (a) and (b) contribute to the third point, which is that Purcell has created an overall shape for this movement, with larger sections made up of several repetitions of the bass line.

These three points could be summarized as

(a) disguising the sections,
(b) varying the repetitions,
(c) creating an overall shape.

Don't worry if you didn't obtain the answers that I arrived at. My reason for asking you the question was to try to put you in the composer's shoes, as it were, to make the point that each piece of music represents a puzzle to be solved by the composer.

Now let us take each of these points in my answer in turn to understand a little more about how this piece 'works'.

DISGUISING THE SECTIONS

If the voice part had followed the sectional nature of the bass part, then Purcell would have been restricted to four-bar phrases (or shorter) for the singer. A brief examination of the score, however, shows that voice part is not restricted in this way. The beginning of the piece is a good example. Rather than entering together with the bass line, the voice part waits until almost the middle of the first four-bar section before coming in. The bass line finishes its first statement of the ground in bar 4, but at this point, the singer is in the middle of the phrase 'Ah! Belinda', and the vocal line does not really come to rest until the end of bar 8, this time coinciding with the end of the second statement of the ground. Indeed, the voice part did not enter until bar 2, which means that its first phrase is 7 bars long instead of the 4 or 8 that we might expect – another irregularity. A similar technique is found a few bars later. Starting at bar 13, the bass part has its usual four-bar repetition of the bass theme, but at the same time the voice part begins a phrase that will last for five bars. Harmonically, this section is also interesting. So far in the piece, we have been used to the first note of the bass theme being accompanied by a chord of C minor (the first beats of bars 1, 5 and 9). In bar 13, however, a chord of C minor would be difficult because of the D in the voice part. Purcell's choice is a type of chord that you have not yet met in this course. Don't worry about its correct description now; the important point to note is that a chord of C minor is replaced by something else here. This, then, is a further example of irregularity in this piece. There are many other similar examples as the music progresses.

LISTEN TO BARS 1–17 OF ITEM 5 AGAIN BEFORE READING ON.

VARYING THE REPETITIONS

Purcell keeps to his strict four-bar repetition pattern in the bass part to the end of bar 28. At this point there is an abrupt change. Instead of bar 29 starting with a C, it begins with a G. The melodic shape of the bass in bars 29–32 is an exact repetition of bars 1–4, except that each note is played an interval of a fourth lower i.e. the complete bass part is transposed a fourth lower. This is repeated in bars 33–6, and followed by a return to a statement of the bass theme in the tonic at bar 37. Here we have another example of

Purcell's irregular treatment of the form; but it is precisely this 'bending of the rules' that prevents the work becoming monotonous.

CREATING ON OVERALL SHAPE

This aria could have been merely a succession of short four-bar sections but because of its length Purcell has given it a larger-scale structure:

Section A   Bars 1–17 (repeated)
Section B   Subsection X. Bars 18–28 including two almost identical statements of the vocal phrase 'Peace and I are strangers grown'.
            Subsection Y. Bars 29–47 including the two different statements of the bass part discussed above.
            Subsection X. Bars 48 to the end, beginning with two statements of the phrase 'Peace and I are strangers grown' followed by a short orchestral passage to close the movement.

Make sure that you have noted all the 'events' in this table (and perhaps marked them in your score), especially the internal 'XYX' structure of section B.

Now listen to 'Ah! Belinda' again, following it in your score, being careful to note all of the factors discussed above.

LISTEN AGAIN TO ITEM 5 AND FOLLOW YOUR SCORE.

4 VARIATION FORMS

The grounds that you have just been studying represent one type of variation structure – the sort in which the bass line is the only constant factor. The popularity of this form declined rapidly in the eighteenth century, with very few examples composed after about 1750. After that time another type of variation came to the fore (though it had been used earlier). Rather than numerous repetitions of a single phrase, these other variations were usually based on longer sections. Very few have themes less than eight bars in length, and sixteen or thirty-two bar sections are not unusual. Because of this, the total number of variations in any one set is often relatively small (up to a dozen or so), although there are some notable exceptions (for example, J. S. Bach's 30 'Goldberg' Variations and Beethoven's 33 'Diabelli' Variations). Unlike grounds, these works are almost always termed 'Variations' (or 'Theme and Variations').

A set of variations almost always begins with a theme. This theme usually consists of three important elements: (i) a melody, with (ii) harmony, over (iii) a bass line. Sometimes, there is just a melody and a bass line, and occasionally only one of these elements is used. In all but a very few works, at least one element remains constant in each variation, although it may be a different element in successive variations (or a particularly characteristic feature of an element, such as rhythm only, might be retained). In other words, any variation has to be recognizably the same as the theme in some respect at least (obviously, because otherwise it would cease to be a *variation!*).

Look now in Scores 2 (p.33) at the second movement of the Keyboard Sonata in A major, Hob. XVI:30, by Joseph Haydn,[1] dating from 1776. This movement is a set of variations. At this time sets of variations were particularly popular, especially with composers for the keyboard, and they remained so for at least another half-century. The direction 'Tempo di Menuet' at the beginning of the piece simply means 'the speed of a Menuet'. The 'Menuet' (commonly also spelt 'Minuet', 'Menuetto', and other ways too) was the most popular of all dances at the time. It was so popular that it found its way regularly into the symphony and sonata, and numerous individual works with the title exist for various instruments and ensembles. This piece, then, is a set of variations on a minuet. The minuet itself is presumably by Haydn, but there is no reason why the composer should not have 'borrowed' it from another composer: it was common practice to write a set of variations on a theme by someone else. (Beethoven's 'Diabelli' variations are good examples of this, using as their basis a Waltz by the Viennese composer and publisher Anton Diabelli.)

Which keyboard instrument did the composer have in mind? There are four possible answers: the organ, harpsichord, clavichord or piano. The absence of dynamics might suggest the organ or harpsichord, neither of which is touch-sensitive – that is, the volume is not affected by the amount of press-

[1] 'Hob.XVI:30' refers to the number in A. van Hoboken's catalogue of Haydn's works.

ure exerted on the keys. Composers, though, were not always conscientious in marking dynamics. There was often no need to include them if the piece was to be played by the composer or a pupil – so the absence of dynamics is not necessarily an indication of the organ or harpsichord. The clavichord is a possibility, since it was a popular domestic instrument. Alternatively, the piano was becoming known all over Europe at this time and may have been used, although there is no evidence that the court at which Haydn worked owned such an instrument by then. A copy of Mozart's piano, made for him by Anton Walter in the early 1780s, is used for the recording of this piece.

Exercise

Listen to the Haydn variations (Audio-cassette Item 6), following the music in your score. We will examine the first three variations in detail here, but I would like you to listen to the complete piece to get a feel for it as a whole. What are the main differences between each of the variations and how are they achieved?

LISTEN TO ITEM 6 AND FOLLOW THE SCORE.

My answer

As with Purcell's Ground in G major, the main differences are in texture and rhythm. Some variations have one note at a time in each hand (two-part writing), others have two notes in one hand and one in the other (three-part writing) and some have a mixture of these textures. At the same time, some variations move predominantly in quavers, while others are largely made up of semiquavers. No attempt is made to disguise the beginnings and ends of sections (as it was in 'Ah! Belinda'): this is normal in variation form (although some composers run two variations together at the end).

Exercise

Now look closely at Variation 1. In what sense is it a variation, i.e. which factors from the theme remain unchanged and which have been altered? Consider both the right- and left-hand parts.

My answer

Apart from the first note, the left-hand part is unchanged. The right hand, however, has changed, and the duration of the note in bar 3 has altered considerably, but not so much as to make it completely unrecognizable. In bar 1 of the variation, for example, the first notes of beats one and two are C♯ and E respectively, just as they were in the theme. In bar 2, the two important notes of both theme and variation are E and D♯. In bar three of Variation 1, Haydn has woven a pattern around the original notes at this point (the notes of the theme are ringed in Example 8).

Example 8 Bar 3 of Variation 1

So it goes on for the rest of the variation: Haydn continues to follow the contours of his theme while adding ornamental notes around it. These become increasingly interesting in the second half of the variation, where there are more chromatic notes (notes which are foreign to the key of the piece at that point as, for example, the B♮ and D♮ of bar 10 of the variation) and at least one rather erratic melodic shape (bar 11).

If I were summarizing Haydn's approach in this variation, I would say that the bass line and harmony were virtually unchanged while the melody was ornamented, or decorated.

Listen to the Theme and Variation 1 again (following them in your score). They are recorded separately as audio-cassette Item 7.

LISTEN NOW TO ITEM 7.

Exercise

What is Haydn's approach in the second variation?

LISTEN TO ITEM 8 AND FOLLOW THE SCORE.

My answer

The first thing that you probably noticed is that the melody of the theme is used in this variation, at least for most of the time. This time, however, it is an octave lower and in the left hand (starting with the higher of the two notes in bar 1 of Variation 2). Apart from being an octave lower, it remains virtually unchanged for the first five bars. In bar 6 of Variation 2, the rhythm of the left hand is the same as the original version in the theme, but the pitches have been raised by one step. In bar 7 of the variation, the rhythm of the right-hand part is the same as the corresponding right-hand part of the theme and in bar 8 the C♯–B of the theme is heard an octave lower in the right hand. Haydn, then, has still kept his original melody, but has played it (slightly altered) in a different **register** (in this case an octave lower). The approach in the second half of the variation is the same.

Two other things are happening in this variation. First, some new musical material appears in the right-hand part of bars 1–4 as well as the beginning of the second half. Secondly, the bass part is altered. This alteration does not amount to much in bars 1, 2 and 4 of the variation. In bars 1 and 4, Haydn has simply lengthened the original bass notes to fill the whole bar. In bar 2, he has selected the B and omitted the A (the less significant of the two notes), and sounded it for the whole bar. But what about bar 3? Why has Haydn replaced the G♯ in the bass line of the theme at this point with an E? The answer lies with the harmony. In bar 3 of the original theme there were two notes at the beginning of the first beat; G♯ in the left hand and B in the right hand. Two notes on their own like this do not form a full chord. On the other hand, there are not very many major or minor chords that they could be part of. We could, therefore, say that they **imply** a certain chord. Whichever chord they imply will be defined by the context of these notes: in this case, the piece is in A major, and we are about to return to an A in the bass of bar 4, so that the chord implied in bar 3 is E major (E, G♯, B) – the dominant (chord V) of A major (you may like to refer back to your A major chord card) and the chord that will help form a perfect cadence between bars 3 and 4 (if we also take the A in bar 4 to imply A major, which is not unreasonable at the end of the first phrase). Don't worry if you found this explanation difficult or impossible to follow at this stage; you may just have to take my word for it that the **implied** harmony of bar 3 of the theme is E major! Or, if your keyboard is to hand, you could add an E between the two notes on the first beat of this bar in the theme to see if it fits.

Turning back to Variation 2, bar 3, you will see that the bass note in the bar is an E – the root of the implied harmony at the equivalent place in the theme. Haydn has therefore retained the harmony of the original but changed the bass line. In bars 5 and 6 of Variation 2, the bass part has disappeared altogether, but it returns, an octave lower than in the theme, in bar 7. A similar treatment of the bass part occurs in the second half of the variation.

To summarize Haydn's approach in Variation 2, we could say three things:

(a) the melody is retained, though altered and played in a different register,

(b) the bass line is altered and is sometimes absent altogether,

(c) the harmony remains the same.

Listen again to Variation 2 and then go on to Variation 3 (Item 9).

Exercise

What is Haydn's approach in the third variation?

LISTEN TO ITEM 9 AND FOLLOW THE SCORE.

My answer

I hope you will see that only some sections of the melody are retained in this variation (for example, bars 2 and 4). Still less of the bass line is retained (for example bars 1 and 3). The implied harmonies that are used, however, remain the same.

A similar mixture of approaches is used in the rest of this set of variations. You might like to spend some time examining the remaining ones, asking similar questions to those above. In any event, you should now listen through to the whole piece again a couple of times (Item 6). As you do so, notice also that Haydn increases the rhythmic activity and variety of the figuration (the melodic and rhythmic patterns into which the notes fall) in variations 4 and 5, as he moves further away from the original shape of the melody in order to sustain the listener's interest in much the same way as Purcell did in his Ground in G major.

LISTEN TO ITEM 6 AND FOLLOW THE SCORE.

By now, I think, the point has been made that there is no single way in which a composer will go about varying a theme. Indeed, the variety of approach to a theme is the essence of variation form. There are, nevertheless, techniques such as melodic elaboration which are common to a great many variations, and certain factors remain common to almost all works in this form:

1. There are three essential factors which can be varied; melody, harmony, bass line.
2. At least one of these factors will remain more or less unchanged during a variation.
3. Variety of texture and rhythm will usually be an important element in the work as a whole.

CONCLUSION AND CHECKLIST

In the first part of this unit I have outlined three types of variation technique:

1. ostinato,
2. ground bass,
3. variation form (or theme and variations).

Before you continue with the rest of the unit, make sure that you are clear about the differences between these three types.

PART 2   BINARY AND TERNARY FORMS

Binary and ternary forms are two of the most important ways of structuring music in the period covered by this course. Their development over the centuries also gives us a great deal of insight into the changing ways in which composers worked. Yet, in essence, both types of form are very simple. As their names suggest, the two forms are defined by the number of sections into which the music falls – two in the case of binary and three in the case of ternary. Between them, they account for a very large proportion of music written in the seventeenth, eighteenth and nineteenth centuries, ranging from the simple teaching piece lasting for less than a minute to symphonic movements of a quarter of an hour or more.

5   TERNARY FORMS

Example 9 (overleaf) is another Minuet, this time by Jean-Philippe Rameau (1683–1764). Rameau was an almost exact contemporary of J. S. Bach and Handel. He was born just two years earlier than both of them and died a little later (Bach died in 1750, Handel in 1759). He was a central figure in French music, both as a composer of operas and as a theoretical writer on music. His lifetime coincided with a very important phase in French keyboard writing; the culmination of a school of harpsichord music that had its origins in the middle of the previous century. Rameau made several important contributions to the keyboard literature of the time, publishing a number of collections of works between 1706 (his *Premier Livre*, 'first book') and 1741 (*Cinq Pièces* – 'five pieces'). Example 9 comes from the preface to his 1724 collection, which also contains observations and instructions on harpsichord performance. (You can see some of these instructions in Scores 2, p.53, where this piece is reproduced as it was originally printed.)

The full title of Rameau's minuet is *Menuet en Rondeau*. It gives us more than a hint of what to expect in the form of the piece. The French composed many of their works 'en Rondeau'. The term means that a section within the work is repeated. Outside France similar forms were also used, generally bearing the name 'Rondo'. All such forms usually start with a section which can be labelled 'A' and continue with other, contrasting sections which then alternate with A to form an overall pattern such as ABACA, or ABACADA.

Example 9 *Rameau's* Menuet en Rondeau

[musical score of Rameau's Menuet en Rondeau, with "fin" marked at bar 8]

In the case of Example 9, the A section recurs only once, so the form is ABA – a ternary form.

Look at the score of Rameau's *Minuet*. You will notice that it has the markings 𝄋 written above the staves at the beginning and the end, and the word **fin** (French for 'end', similar to the Italian 'fine') in bar 8. These are performance directions which mean that, after bar 16, the player should return to the beginning and repeat the music down to the word **fin**, the end of the piece.

Exercise

Listen to Example 9 now (Item 10), following the music and asking two questions:

(a) Which bars correspond to the A and B sections of this ternary (ABA) form?

(b) How are the sections contrasted?

LISTEN TO ITEM 10 AND FOLLOW EXAMPLE 9.

My answer

The answer to (a) is straightforward. The form of the piece divides like this:

A   bars 1–8

B   bars 9–16

A   bars 1–8 (repeated).

Rameau has even put a double barline at the end of each section to make the form clear. If you didn't get this question right, then listen to the piece again, following my plan of the form.

The answer to (b) is more difficult. If you look closely at the right-hand part of bars 1 and 9 you will notice that the melodic shape is the same (that is, the intervals between successive notes in bar 9 are the same as those in bar 1). The right-hand part of bar 9, then, is the same as bar 1, except that it has been transposed a fourth lower. The same is true for the rest of the section: bars 9–16 are the same as bars 1–8, but a fourth lower. What about the left hand part? It doesn't look the same as bar 1 because of the sharp sign before the F; but in fact it is this sharp that gives it the same shape as bar 1, because it ensures that the interval between the last two notes of the bar is a semitone, just as it was in bar 1. The left-hand part of bar 9, then, is the same as that of bar 1, except it is a fourth lower, and that pattern is continued until bar 16, which, however, is not quite the same as bar 8.

In summary, bars 9–16 are the same as bars 1–8 (apart from the left-hand part of bar 16), except that they are transposed down a fourth. What this means is that we have gone into a new key for this section, the key of G major (the dominant of C major – the key formed on the fifth, or dominant, note of the C major scale). You can test this assertion by referring back to Unit 6. In the video section of that unit it was explained that the scale of C major included all of the white notes on the keyboard and no others. A section of music using these notes was said to be in the key of C major. If, however, we wanted to play a scale with all the tones and semitones in the same order starting on the note G, then instead of the ordinary white note, F, we would need to play an F♯. This is another way of saying that a scale of G major has F♯ instead of F♮. Similarly, a section of music which uses the notes of the G major scale can be said to be in the key of G major (see Unit 6, Section 8.2).

Returning to Rameau's minuet, we can see that bars 1–8 involve only the notes of the C major scale. This section of the piece is therefore in C major. From bar 9 to the beginning of bar 16, however, there are no F♮s, only F♯s. This section of the piece is therefore in the key of G major. That just leaves the last few notes of bar 16, which include an F♮ in the left-hand part, whose function is to lead us back to the beginning of the piece, in C major again.

We can now be more specific about the form of this minuet:

A	bars 1–8	C major	(tonic key)
B	bars 9–16	G major	(dominant key)
A	bars 1–8 (repeated)	C major	(tonic key)

You may be wondering why, if bars 9–16 are in G major, there is no new key signature for those bars. The reason is that composers write a new key signature only if the music is going to be in the new key for a substantial time. Otherwise, the key of the piece as a whole (that is, the key in which the piece starts and finishes) is reflected in the key signature.

Listen to the minuet once more, following it in your score, and check that you have understood the points above. Then listen to another recording of it, which is given as Item 11. You will notice in this second recording that the quavers within each beat are not played equally. This follows a performance convention of the time, the practice of notes **inégales** ('unequal notes'), which was supposed to lend a certain grace or elegance to a piece by the unequal playing of quavers, or sometimes semiquavers.

LISTEN TO ITEM 11 AND FOLLOW EXAMPLE 9.

Rameau's *Menuet en Rondeau* illustrates a very important principle in a great deal of Western music – that form can be defined by the use of keys. It is true of almost all (if not all) ternary forms and a number of other different structures too. We will be returning to this principle later in this unit and in many places later in the course.

Before we leave ternary form for the moment, look back to the Scherzo and Trio from Beethoven's Piano Sonata Op. 2 No. 2 in Scores 2 (p.20). This is an example of ternary form on a larger scale. Whatever the internal divisions of the Scherzo and Trio, you will remember that in performance the piece follows this sequence: Scherzo–Trio–Scherzo (ABA). As in Rameau's minuet, the key scheme is an important element in the way in which the sections are divided:

Scherzo	A major
Trio	A minor
Scherzo	A major

Because it is a longer and more complex piece, the contrast between sections does not depend on key alone; Beethoven uses different textures as well. Yet, despite the very different character of this piece, not to mention its length, it remains in the same basic form as Rameau's: it is still in ternary form. Incidentally, you may have noticed that Beethoven *does* change the key signature for the B section, because it is a much longer section than Rameau's.

Beethoven's use of the scherzo in this sonata is quite unusual for its time (1795). Conventionally, it was the minuet rather than the scherzo that was used in one of the middle movements of a sonata or symphony. When a minuet was used, however, it was often part of a larger structure, minuet-trio-minuet, in a similar manner to the scherzo and trio from Beethoven's Sonata in A major.

If you wish to listen to Beethoven's Scherzo and Trio, you will find it as Unit 9, audio-cassette Item 12.

6 BINARY FORMS

Binary forms have two sections: beyond that it is not all that easy to generalize, since composers treat the form in such a variety of ways! The rest of this unit introduces you to some of the most important issues relating to pieces in that form.

You have already been introduced to J. S. Bach's notebook for his second wife, Anna Magdalena, in Unit 9. Almost all of the fifty or so works in the collection are in binary form, easily recognizable by the repeat signs which normally occur somewhere in the middle of each piece. The reason why there is such a high proportion of binary forms is because most of the pieces are dances of one type or another; and most eighteenth-century dances have two sections, each of which is repeated. Example 10 is perhaps the simplest of all the pieces in the collection. It has no title, but is clearly in binary form, each of the two sections being of almost equal length (7 and 8 bars respectively).

Note: this piece begins with an **anacrusis** – an incomplete bar (with only one beat in it). It is customary in such pieces to include a correspondingly incomplete bar at the end, and to count the first *complete* bar as bar 1.

Exercise

Example 10 is recorded as Item 12. Listen to it and follow Example 10.

(a) What key is the piece in?
(b) What key does the first section end in (i.e. at the double bar)?

Example 10

LISTEN TO ITEM 12 AND FOLLOW EXAMPLE 10.

My answer and discussion

There might have been two answers to the first question: a key signature of one flat is used in both F major and D minor (see Unit 6, Section 9.7). If the piece had been in D minor, however, we would have expected the final bass note to be a D, and the first notes of the piece to belong to the chord of D minor (D, F, A) or its dominant (chord V of that key), the chord of A major (A, C♯, E). Neither is the case here. We would also expect to see some C♯s, the leading note of D minor; but there are none. Moreover, the final bass note is F, and the opening notes of the piece in both hands are C and F. The piece is therefore in F major.

The answer to question (b) is C major. Where does the music begin to leave F major for C major? The answer is in bar 5. This is the first time that a B♭ is replaced by a B♮. Thereafter, for the rest of the first section, there are no B♭s, and the G to C progression in the bass line of bars 6 to 7 is that of a perfect cadence in C major.

C major does not last for long. The second half of the piece almost immediately reintroduces the B♭s, taking us back to F major. The form of the piece is therefore:

| A | bars 1–7 | tonic to dominant |
| B | bars 8–15 | back to the tonic |

We can call the form of this short piece an **open** binary form, since the first section ends in a different key from the one in which it began. (A closed binary form would be one in which the first section began and ended in the tonic. You will find an example later in this section.)

Listen to the piece once more, following it in Example 10; only this time listen to the recording of it in Item 13. This version has added ornamentation (following practices described in Unit 9) since it would otherwise be rather dull.

LISTEN NOW TO ITEM 13.

My analysis of Example 10 might give the impression that the keys are the most vital elements and that everything else is of little importance. Yet if you listen to the piece a few times, it is probably the melody line, or one or two fragments of it, that you will remember. Does that mean to say that keys are not so important after all? The answer, I think, is that the keys and the melody line (and other elements in the music as well) serve different functions, in the same way that different parts of a building serve different functions. The parts of a building that provide its strength (foundations and main structural supports) are often hidden, or unremarkable in appearance, whereas the more memorable parts of a building (carvings, staircases, windows, etc.) serve little or no structural purpose. Likewise, the key scheme of a piece of music may have little or no impact on the listener (who is more likely to be drawn to an interesting melodic line, or dramatic increase in dynamics, etc.) yet it is often the foundation or structure on which the piece is built. Any analysis of a binary form (and other forms too) will therefore have to take into account the key scheme in order to grasp the underlying structure on which the composer has built the piece.

Exercise

Look at the G major Polonaise by J. S. Bach in Scores 2 (p.8). Remind yourself of it by listening to Item 14. The repeat signs at the end of bar 8 clearly divide the piece into the two sections of a binary form. What key is the music in at the following points?

(a) In bar 8.

(b) At the beginning of bar 16.

LISTEN TO ITEM 14 AND FOLLOW THE SCORE.

My answer

(a) G major. There have been no additional sharps or flats in the music, so there is no reason to suppose that the key has changed since the beginning of the piece, which was in G major. The bass line in bar 8 supports this view: it progresses from D to G, the V–I progression of a perfect cadence in G major.

(b) D major. Beginning at bar 9, after the first chord, C♯ has consistently replaced C♮. It is not, however, until bar 16 that the music comes to rest with a cadence (the progression A-D in the bass line at the beginning of bar 16 is that of a perfect cadence in D major). That is the reason why I asked you for the key at this point rather than in any of the preceding bars.

The form of this Polonaise can be summarized in the following way:

A	bars 1–8	G major
B	bars 9–28	Going very quickly from G major to D major, returning to G major.

It is a **closed** binary form (since the first section begins and ends in the same key). In the Polonaise, the second section of the piece contains the important 'events' relating to key, which explains why that section takes more than two thirds of the total length of the piece (although we may still refer to it as the second 'half'). Compare this with Example 10 of this unit, where the 'events' were evenly spread between the two sections, which is why they are roughly equal in length. It is clear from these two pieces that the key scheme in binary form may vary, and that it will affect the internal proportions of each work. There is, however, at least one feature belonging to both of these examples which is common to almost all examples of this form in major keys from the seventeenth to the nineteenth centuries; sooner or later they move, or *modulate*, to the dominant, returning to the tonic at the end. (In minor key pieces the equivalent procedure is to modulate to the relative major before returning to the tonic at the end.) In the first half of the eighteenth century the place where the modulation to the dominant happens within the movement appears not to have been fixed but in the second half of the century it almost invariably occurs in the middle of the first section, as we shall see in a moment. Modulation (the process of changing key) is an important concept which you will study in detail in Unit 13.

Before we leave Bach's G major *Polonaise*, I would like to draw your attention to a few more points. Having said (earlier in this section) that the key scheme was the underlying structure in binary forms I would not like to leave you with the impression that composers always try to conceal it. Sometimes, it is true, the key scheme passes almost unnoticed, but on other occasions modulations to and from keys coincide with other musical events, bringing the structure to the surface. This is particularly true in the music of the Classical era (roughly 1750–1820) which we will be considering shortly.

It is also true in some measure in Bach's Polonaise in G major. Adding a little more information to my analysis, we could define the structure as follows:

A	bars 1–8	G major
B	bars 9–16	Modulating to, and establishing, D major.
	bars 16–20	Modulating back to G major.
	bars 21–8	G major

I have used the terms 'modulating to' and 'modulating back' in my analysis because a new key is not established immediately we hear the relevant sharps or flats: it takes time and the process of modulation usually ends with a perfect cadence in the new key. In bar 9, for example, the introduction of a C♯ in the right-hand part does not immediately make us feel that we have modulated to a new key. This is because we have just had sixteen bars of G major (the first section is repeated) which has firmly established that key in our minds. It will take a little while for the memory of G major to be wiped out and a new key firmly established.

Now look at the actual musical material that Bach uses. When you studied this piece in Unit 9, you noted certain events that recurred in the piece such as the passage in bars 5 and 6 where the two hands play the same music an octave apart and the high note followed by a downward scale in bars 7 and 8. The two events follow one another and recur in bars 13–16 and 25–8. These are the passages which lead to the final cadence in each of the key areas shown in my structural table above. In other words, their place in the piece has been planned to coincide with important events relating to key. Similarly, bars 21 and 22, the beginning of the final section in the home key, have a prominent feature in common with the opening two bars of the piece, that is, the repeated Gs in the left-hand part. There is therefore a certain symmetry in the way that the opening and closing G major sections of the piece begin with similar material.

7 THE SONATA PRINCIPLE

Two of J. S. Bach's sons, Carl Philipp Emanuel (1714–88) and Johann Christian (1735–82), were very important in the development of binary form in the middle of the eighteenth century. In their works (and in the music of a number of their contemporaries) a more regular approach to the key scheme emerged, so that the majority of binary-form movements in major keys from the second half of the eighteenth century follow this pattern in outline:

A	‖: Tonic	Dominant :‖
B	‖: Various keys	Tonic :‖

Minor-key works follow a similar scheme:

A	‖: Tonic	Relative Major :‖
B	‖: Various keys	Tonic :‖

These alternative key schemes are followed by numerous works of the period which are based on the **sonata principle**. This is one of the most important structural principles of Western European art music, which you will be returning to in a number of later units in this course. For the moment, I simply want to introduce it to you: other authors will explain it in more detail.

Figure 1 J. C. Bach. Portrait attributed to Thomas Gainsborough, 1780.

Exercise

Look at your score of the first movement of J. C. Bach's Sonata in D major Op. 5 No. 2 (in Scores 2, p. 14). It follows the pattern laid out above for major-key sonata-principle works. Before you listen to the piece, try to identify the important key areas. You will probably find this difficult on account of the piece's length, but spend a little while on this part of the exercise nevertheless. Remember that D major has a key signature of two sharps (F♯ and C♯). Its dominant, A major, has an additional sharp in its key signature: G♯.

Spend a few minutes on this now, and then listen to the movement (Item 15), following the music in your score. (In case they confuse you, 'po' and 'fe' are abbreviations for 'piano' and 'forte', dynamic markings you are already familiar with.)

LISTEN TO ITEM 15 AND FOLLOW THE SCORE.

Answer

The end of the first section (bar 42) is in A major – there is a perfect cadence (V–I) here which confirms that this is the case. But I don't expect you found it very easy to be precise about where the music goes into the dominant in the first section. The first G♯ appears in bar 9, but the music does not feel very settled for the following few bars. In bar 19, however, the music settles down in the new key (there is a V–I progression from bar 18 to bar 19) and it remains there for the rest of the section. Likewise, in the second section, it is not very easy to be precise about where the music returns to the tonic. There are several G♯s, beginning at bar 48, but at the same time there are D♯s and A♯s (bar 51).

This passage is in fact in B minor (though it touches on other keys in a couple of places, hence the D♯s), corresponding with the section labelled 'various keys' in my scheme above. There are two perfect cadences in B minor in bars 51/52 and bars 59/60. In bar 65, however, we begin to have whole bars of notes belonging just to D major (though even then, bar 68, with its G♯s, temporarily reminds us of A major). Finally, in bar 73, the music settles firmly in the home key.

My analysis of the key scheme for this movement looks like this:

A	bars 1–8	D major
	bars 9–18	Moving to A major.
	bars 19–42	A major
B	bars 43–64	'Various'
	bars 65–72	Preparing us for D major.
	bars 73–end	D major.

The interesting point about this structure, compared with other pieces we have examined in this unit, is that it is not in any sense hidden, or secondary to other events in the music. Quite the reverse is true. The transitions from one key to another in fact provide much of the drama of the piece. In the first section, for example, when the music begins to move away from D major at bar 9, we enter a rather turbulent passage, with strong rhythms and busy semiquavers. At the end of this passage, both hands have one beat's rest (bar 18) before the relaxation, in the next bar, into the dominant key of A major. With the arrival of the new key we also have new musical material – in this case a melody in the right hand. We can therefore divide the first section of the piece ('A' in my analysis above) at bar 19 into two distinct groups, which make up the 'exposition' of this movement. The **Exposition** in sonata-principle movement is thus the first section, containing material in the tonic and dominant (or relative major if the tonic is minor), usually ending with a repeat sign.

A similarly important harmonic event occurs in the second half of the movement, between bars 65 and 72: we are kept in suspense by the repeated A in the left hand. Clearly something important is about to happen. When it does, it is the return of the tonic, D major, in bar 73, and to emphasize the importance of this moment, we also have a return of the opening bars of the piece.

Listen to the music once again, following these events in your score.

LISTEN AGAIN TO ITEM 15 AND FOLLOW THE SCORE.

Now let's take a closer look at the second half of the piece. The section of music in bars 43–72 has at its centre another rather turbulent passage, and the keys of the whole section change at a faster rate than elsewhere in the movement – in this section we start with A major, going on to several bars in B minor, then passing through G major and A major again before the end of bar 64.

These two features, turbulence and movement through several keys, are often common to this phase of a sonata-principle movement. It is usually referred to as the '**development**' section, since it is the part of the movement where some musical ideas from the exposition may be re-shaped – but more of this in later units.

At bar 73, as I mentioned earlier, we returned to the opening music of the piece. In fact, if you follow the rest of the movement through, you will see that it contains the rest of the music of the exposition. This time, however, we do not modulate to the dominant (A major) for the second group of musical material, but stay in the tonic throughout. This phase of the form is usually referred to as the '**recapitulation**'. It is the part of the movement where the tensions of the previous sections are resolved.

We can now be more specific about the form of this movement:

A	Exposition	Bars 1–18	‖: First group in the tonic, with transition to:
		Bars 19–42	second group, in the dominant. :‖
B	Development	Bars 43–72	‖: Development section, using various keys, with preparation for:
	Recapitulation	Bars 73 to end.	both groups in the tonic. :‖

The essence of the sonata principle as demonstrated in this movement, then, is its clearly-articulated key scheme - a relatively simple key scheme that forms the basis for the drama of the work. This structure (and its minor-key version) is shared by thousands of movements composed in the eighteenth and nineteenth centuries. It is capable of infinite variation and proved to be an extremely important structure.

Writers on music, too, have found it an endless source of fascination – books about it continue to appear frequently. Much more will be said about it later in this course, but for the moment (and as an apt way of ending a unit which deals with binary and ternary forms) I would like to leave you with one question to consider. If you remove the second repeat, and hear the development and recapitulation only once, does the form remain binary, or does it become ternary? The question is not a hypothetical one. From Beethoven's time onwards the B section of the form grew in length, which led to the disappearance of the second repeat in many sonata forms of the nineteenth century. Musicians, therefore, who study the form in music of that period tend to encounter the question sooner or later. Whether or not they agree on an answer is another matter.

8 SUMMARY

In this part of the unit I have outlined various types of binary and ternary forms:

1. ternary forms,
2. binary forms,
3. the sonata principle.

Make sure that you have understood these terms, and that you are aware of the difference between open and closed binary/ternary forms. You will also remember that there was a brief checklist at the end of Part I which included the following:

1. ostinato,
2. ground bass,
3. variation form (or theme and variations)

There has been a good deal of demanding analysis this week some of which you will have found difficult. But if you have grasped the important features of the various forms that have been discussed, you will have achieved the aims of this unit.

ACKNOWLEDGEMENTS

Figure 1   Liceo Musicale G.B. Martini, Bologna. Photo: Mansell-Alinari.

Example 2   Éditions Durand S. A. Copyright Durand & Cie., 1929.

Example 4   Stainer and Bell Ltd.

Example 10   Bärenreiter-Verlag Karl Vötterle GmbH & Co.

REFERENCE MATERIAL

SOME TERMS AND SIGNS

VOLUME

pianissimo (pp)	very soft
piano (p)	soft
mezzo forte (mf)	moderately loud
forte (f)	loud
fortissimo (ff)	very loud
cresecendo (cresc.)	becoming louder
⟨	becoming louder
diminuendo (dim.)	becoming softer
decrescendo (decresc.)	becoming softer
⟩	becoming softer

TEMPO AND STYLE

grave	very slowly
adagio	slowly
largo	broadly
larghetto	fairly broadly
andante	walking pace
moderato	moderate speed
allegretto	moderately fast
allegro	fast, lively
presto	very fast
prestissimo	as fast as possible
vivace	lively
accellerando (accel.)	become faster
allargando (allarg.)	become broader
rallentando (rall.)	slowing down
ritardando (rit.)	slowing down
ritenuto	holding back
stringendo (string.)	moving on
tempo primo	back to original speed
a tempo	back to original speed

MISCELLANEOUS

‖: :‖	repeat
⌒	pause (fermata)
sforzando (sf)	accent
♩ (>)	accent
♩.	staccato (short)
Da Capo (D.C.)	return to the beginning
Dal Segno (D.S.)	return to the sign 𝄋
Fine	the end

MAJOR AND MINOR IN PRINCIPAL EUROPEAN LANGUAGES

	Minor	Major
Eng.	minor	major
Fr.	mineur	majeur
Ger.	moll	dur
It.	minore	maggiore
Sp.	menor	mayor

FORM DIAGRAMS I; BINARY AND TERNARY FORMS

Keys in brackets show what happens in minor-key versions of the form.

CLOSED BINARY

For example, J. S. Bach's Polonaise in G major from the Anna Magdalena Bach book.

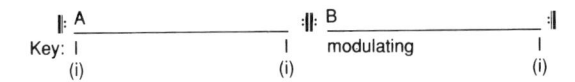

```
     ‖: A               :‖: B                      :‖
Key:  I                 I   modulating              I
     (i)               (i)                         (i)
```

OPEN BINARY

For example, J. C. Bach's Keyboard Sonata in D, Op. 5 No. 2.

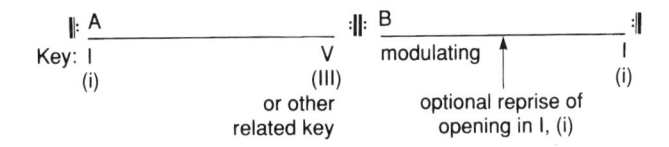

```
     ‖: A                       :‖: B                      :‖
Key:  I                          V   modulating             I
     (i)                       (III)                       (i)
                             or other    optional reprise of
                            related key  opening in I, (i)
```

Note. If there is the optional reprise shown in part B, the form is known as **rounded binary** (see Unit 24).

For the **sonata principle**, an extension of open binary form, see Units 10, 18 and 28.

TERNARY, OR DA CAPO ARIA FORM

For example, Rameau's *Menuet en Rondeau*.

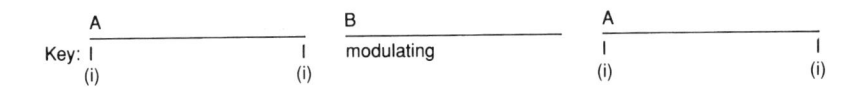

```
      A                  B                  A
Key:  I        I         modulating    I              I
     (i)      (i)                     (i)            (i)
```

A214 UNDERSTANDING MUSIC: ELEMENTS, TECHNIQUES AND STYLES

Unit 1	Introducing rhythm	Unit 17	Harmonizing a melody I
Unit 2	More about rhythm; Introducing pitch	Unit 18	Modulation II
Unit 3	Starting with staff notation	Unit 19	Harmonizing a melody II
Unit 4	Melody	Unit 20	Following an orchestral score
Unit 5	Harmony I: The chord	Unit 21	Transpositions and reductions
Unit 6	Modes, scales and keys	Unit 22	Formal principles II
Unit 7	Primary triads	Unit 23	Baroque style study I
Unit 8	Cadences	Unit 24	Classical style study I
Unit 9	Following a score I	Unit 25	Some points of style
Unit 10	Formal principles I	Unit 26	Baroque style study II
		Unit 27	Classical style study II
Unit 11	First inversion chords		
Unit 12	Secondary diatonic triads (II, III, VI and VII)	Unit 28	The Romantic period
Unit 13	Modulation I	Unit 29	Style, history and canon
Unit 14	Following a score II	Unit 30	Baroque style study III
Unit 15	Two-stave reduction	Unit 31	Classical style study III
Unit 16	Mostly revision	Unit 32	Towards the examination: Writing about music